# THE GOD BETWEEN

# THE GOD BETWEEN

CHARLES E. BRADFORD

REVIEW AND HERALD PUBLISHING ASSOCIATION
Washington, DC 20039-0555
Hagerstown, MD 21740

This book was
Edited by Richard W. Coffen
Designed by Richard Steadham
Type set: 11/12 Zapf

PRINTED IN U.S.A.

**Library of Congress Cataloging in Publication Data**

Bradford, Charles E.
The God between.

1. Jesus Christ—Person and offices. 2. Mediation between God and man—Christianity. I. Title.
BT255.B75 1984 234 84-8311

ISBN 0-8280-0243-6

# CONTENTS

# FOREWORD

It has been said that New Testament Greek, the *Koine,* is the richest language of all. Whether or not that claim is true, under the inspiration of the Holy Spirit it became, on the lips and from the pens of human instrumentalities, the vehicle of communication for the unsearchable riches of Christ's gospel. Some words seem ready-made for expressing the great themes of salvation. For example, there are the words *mesos,* which means "in the middle," and *mesitēs,* "the one who stands in the middle"—the mediator. The *mesitēs* takes his position between persons to unite them when they have quarreled or to help them act in harmony when they cannot do so on their own.

There is, in the economy of salvation, one who stands in the middle, Jesus Christ. He is the God between, the "one mediator between God and men" (1 Tim. 2:5). He represents God to human beings and mankind to God and makes peace among fellowmen. Furthermore, the *mesitēs* stands equidistant between parties—no farther or no closer to the one than to the other. "Then I saw in my vision a Lamb standing in the middle of the throne, in the *centre* of the circle of the four living creatures and of the twenty-four elders" (Rev. 5:6, Barclay).

# A SPACE-AGE PARABLE

*Think of a spaceship hurtling through the universe. The passengers feel apprehensive and uneasy, but they do not know the real danger, the terrible predicament, the stark reality, the bleakness of their situation. An evil usurper has taken control, who for some strange reason has a deep hatred for all on board—even the little ones. He is bent on leading them all to destruction, but he is crafty and subtle. He hides his true motives.*

*Then quietly, unobtrusively (it was a "silent night"), another Passenger boards the craft. He looks like any other traveler, and they hardly notice Him. Only a few—a very few—recognize Him. Little by little He makes himself known. He is the rightful owner of the craft. The man at the controls is a pretender prince who took over by deceit and underhanded dealing. The new Voyager explains their predicament. This "Man from Wayout," we may call Him, promises deliverance and salvation. He also asks for their allegiance. "Follow Me," He says.*

*A terrible struggle ensues. Finally He wrests control from the hijacker. It is a Friday afternoon. Then just as soon as the passengers were getting used to Him, He left, but promised, "I'll be back. Keep the faith while I'm away."*

*The story hasn't ended yet. But some believe He will return, and some don't. At any rate, things have not been the same on the spacecraft since His visit.*

# Introduction

"For there is one God, and one mediator between God and men, the man Christ Jesus; who gave himself a ransom for all, to be testified in due time" (1 Tim. 2:5, 6).

This book is about mediation. It is also about the Mediator, Jesus Christ, the absolutely singular. And what is mediation? Defined at its simplest, it is bringing two estranged parties together. But do not let this apparent simplicity mislead you. The idea of mediation permeates all Scripture. The concept is exceedingly broad. It involves God, man, and the universe—all of creation. So we have a doctrine here that on the surface is simple (the apostle Paul catches its essence in two short verses) and at the same time is the very "depth of the riches both of the wisdom and knowledge" and ways of God, which this same apostle calls "unsearchable . . . and . . . past finding out" (Rom. 11:33). Some go so far as to say that the concept of mediation is the most profound idea in the Scriptures—a central organizing principle that is the key to understanding the plan of salvation.

Such claims are rather surprising, because the word *mediation* does not occur in the King James Version, and *mediator* occurs only six times in the New Testament. And yet underlying almost every aspect of the plan of salvation is this idea of the mediator and mediation. Sometimes the word *mediate* is used in the sense of "interpose" or "give a guarantee." (See Hebrews 6:17, where "confirmed" translates the verb for mediate.) In its noun form *mediator* may be translated "negotiator" or "intermediary." Other Biblical references speak of Christ's mediatorial ministry in terms of His effectiveness for man's salvation or His institution of the new covenant under which man and God are brought into right relationship.

We must conclude, therefore, that Christ exercises His mediatorship in all the phases of redemption, from the beginning to end—from the "counsel of peace" that was "between them both" (Zech. 6:13) to the final consummation of salvation when all is accomplished. Jesus Christ is mediator in humiliation and exaltation. His mediatorial activity involves much. It cannot be defined in terms of one idea or function. His mediatorship has as many aspects as does His person, office, and work. A great diversity marks the offices and tasks that Jesus carries out as mediator. His ministry is a multifaceted ministry. We need an intelligent faith when we come to worship Him. We need to recognize this diversity.

The Father has conferred upon Jesus Christ a unique glory, which demands that we give this high place to no other. As Paul has it, there is one Mediator between God and humanity. Jesus Christ stands without a peer. Jesus Christ, then, as mediator becomes the point of contact between heaven and earth, between God and man. He is God's agent. He is our representative. He is prophet, priest, and king. As prophet He mediates the will of God and reveals God to the human family. As priest He takes up our case and becomes our "friend at court." As king He exercises the righteous rule of God, the establishment of the kingdom that is first of all "within you," in the hearts of His followers.

The concept of mediation also has a cosmic dimension. A deep cleavage or rupture mars God's creation. All nature groans. An entire race is quarantined on a doomed planet. The mediation of which we speak, then, must address this very real problem. The energies of the Godhead have been drawn out to meet the emergency. An entire universe has been affected. The work of the Mediator must reach far and wide. Two Scripture texts come to mind. "That in the dispensation of the fulness of times he might gather together in one all things in Christ, both which are in heaven, and which are on earth; even in him" (Eph. 1:10). "And, having made peace through the blood of his cross, by him to reconcile all things unto himself; by him, I say, whether they be things in earth, or things in heaven" (Col. 1:20).

The Mediator *gathers* and *reconciles.* The enemy has scattered and driven away. Sin has a shattering and scattering effect. Because of sin the universe is out of joint. The disunited parts must be brought together again. The situation calls for a mediator. This little book attempts to describe how the Mediator goes about His work. It also tries to make clear what is involved in His work and to portray His special efforts to "get it together," as they say.

The word *reconcile* suggests the personal dimension, the relational. Nature is affected and so are we. Hostility and estrangement abound. The situation calls for a mediator—someone who is trusted and trustworthy, someone to take the initiative, someone who is willing "to go out from his place" (this willingness to go out is an idea that is inferred from the early understanding of the mediatorial function)—to give of himself. Wherever alienation and estrangement lurk, the office of a mediator is required to bring about reconciliation.

Mediation suggests activity. The Mediator *does* something. He is no reclining celestial monarch, at rest, at ease, attended by a host of servants. "He ever liveth to make intercession" (Heb. 7:25). "His mediatory activity is never suspended."—J. D. Douglas, ed., *The New Bible Dictionary,* p. 803. He is always engaged in some phase of priestly ministry—providing forgiveness for sin, cleansing of sin, victory over sin, defense for repentant sinners, and strength for daily living. "As our Mediator, Christ works incessantly. Whether men receive or reject Him, He works earnestly for them. He grants them life and light, striving by His Spirit to win them from Satan's service."—Ellen G. White, in *Review and Herald,* March 12, 1901, quoted in *Questions on Doctrines,* p. 688. His activity does not cease until sin is eradicated and restoration is complete.

The New Testament writers saw this clearly. They knew that only through the effectual work of the Mediator is there a future for humanity and for Planet Earth. This consciousness led them to regard all blessings and benefits as being made available to Christians "through Jesus Christ our Lord." This phrase in one form or another occurs at least twenty-five times in the New Testament. (See John 1:7; 3:17; 20:31; Acts 10:43; Romans 1:8; 3:25; 5:1, 9, 11; 6:11, 23; 7:25; 8:37; 11:36; 15:17; 16:27; 1 Cor. 15:57; 2 Cor. 3:4; Gal. 3:14; 4:7; Eph. 2:7; Phil. 4:13; Titus 3:6; Heb. 13:21; 1 Peter 4:11.)

Christians throughout the centuries have sung the doxology "Praise God, from whom all blessings flow." It is well to keep in mind that the channel or medium through which these blessings reach us, by which they are conveyed, is the "one mediator between God and men, the man Christ Jesus" (1 Tim. 2:5). "Every grace bestowed flows through the channel of Christ's intercession."—*The New Bible Dictionary,* p. 803.

It should comfort and encourage us to know that God has not abandoned His creation. This little planet, which "is only a speck of dust circling round a minor star on the outskirts of one of the lesser galaxies" (John G. Williams, *Christian Faith and the Space Age,* p. 49), called forth His love, His mighty energies, and His deepest thoughts. The Godhead takes up residence in Jesus Christ and through Him reaches out to touch the lost planet. This calls for praise, thanksgiving, and worship. "And I beheld, and I heard . . . many angels round about the throne and the beasts and the elders: . . . saying with a loud voice, Worthy is the Lamb that was slain to receive power, and riches, and wisdom, and strength, and honour, and glory, and blessing. And every creature . . . heard I saying, Blessing, and honour, and glory, and power, be unto him that sitteth upon the throne, and unto the Lamb for ever and ever" (Rev. 5:11-13).

*Introduction to Chapter 1*

# *SHADES OF NIGHT*

*(Apologies to J. B. Phillips.)*

*Close your eyes. Go back in time and space. Imagine: A junior angel and a senior angel stand side by side as they look from the walls of the celestial city into the vast regions of outer space. Stars twinkle, planets whirl in orbit, and constellations and systems move briskly. The junior angel breaks the silence: "What is that strange little planet that looks a bit like a dirty, worn-out tennis ball down there in the Milky Way?"*

*"Why, don't you know? That's earth."*

*"Well, why is it so dark?"*

*"It's because of sin. The archenemy led the planet into rebellion," the senior cherub responds.*

*"Can't something be done about it?" the junior angel asks plaintively, a bit of a tear in his voice. "It's the saddest spot I've seen in the whole universe."*

*"Haven't you heard?" replies the big one. "Our Commander went down and visited that planet. That's why you see those tiny flashes of light piercing the darkness. Because He went down, someday the light will go on again all over the world."*

*Is this fantasy? If it is, it is a fantasy on reality. You and I live on the visited planet. The light has shined in darkness. Light has dawned—"the light of the good news of the glory of Christ, who is exactly like God. . . . It is the God who said: 'Light will shine out of darkness,' who has made his light shine in our hearts to illumine them with the knowledge of the glory of God, seen in the face of Jesus Christ" (2 Cor. 4:4-6, Barclay).*

Chapter 1

# "BEFORE THE WORLD BEGAN"

"Who hath saved us, and called us with an holy calling, not according to our works, but according to his own purpose and grace, which was given us in Christ Jesus *before the world began"* (2 Tim. 1:9). "In hope of eternal life, which God, that cannot lie, promised *before the world began"* (Titus 1:2).

"Before the world began"—in the dim mists of eternity past—an appointment was made and understood. The eternal Son would be the agent of the Godhead, the ambassador plenipotentiary (with unlimited authority) of salvation and redemption. "To wit, that God was in Christ, reconciling the world unto himself" (2 Cor. 5:19). His job description? To bring back the lost planet and to restore fallen creatures to fellowship with Heaven. "For the Son of man is come to seek and to save that which was lost" (Luke 19:10). The time frame? The whole of human history, the measurable span between two eternities. "I am Alpha and Omega, the beginning and the end, the first and the last" (Rev. 22:13).

Only the Hebrew Scriptures have this concept of time as a line rather than a circle. All other ancient philosophies and religious systems talk of cycles, unending, always recurring, *ad infinitum.* What has been will happen again, they thought. History endlessly repeats itself. But the Mediator's assignment has a beginning and an end, a starting point and a finish line. His work is specific in its focus. Mediation has a definite object and clearly defined objectives. All of which was envisioned "from the foundation of the world" (Rev.

13:8). (See also Matt. 13:35; 25:34; Luke 11:50; Eph. 1:4; 1 Peter 1:20.)

The mediatorial ministry of Christ, therefore, includes supervision of the destiny of earth and its inhabitants. As the old spiritual has it, "He's got the whole world in His hands."

Jesus Christ is the administrator and active agent of the plan of salvation. The emphasis here is on performance, achievement. He carries out His Father's instructions. He is sent, commissioned, under orders. "I do nothing of myself." "I speak that which I have seen with my Father." "Neither came I of myself, but he sent me" (John 8:28, 38, 42). The Mediator had an intense consciousness of mission throughout His earthly existence and even before His earthly sojourn. "Then said I, Lo, I come (in the volume of the book it is written of me,) to do thy will, O God" (Heb. 10:7). This is the preexistent Christ speaking. Jesus then became His Father's emissary for carrying out a strategy devised before the foundation of the world. A multitude of responsible functions are given to Jesus as mediator. He is the fully accredited executor of God's decisions.

A world is conceived in the mind of God. Jesus then speaks that world into existence. "For he spake, and it was done; he commanded, and it stood fast" (Ps. 33:9). Before the world was, Christ held eternal communion with the Father and the Holy Spirit. (God is one, but He is manifest in three distinct persons.) All things are laid out plainly by the eternal Trio. Each has perfect knowledge. Now it becomes the Son's duty to bring it all to pass. "For by him were all things created, that are in heaven, and that are in earth, visible and invisible, whether they be thrones, or dominions, or principalities, or powers: all things were created by him, and for him: and he is before all things, and by him all things consist" (Col. 1:16, 17). Nothing is left out, visible or invisible, all kinds of power structures and relationships. The laws of nature came into being at His command, and they continue to exist by that same power. The creation is not a clock wound up and running on its own power. It is not a perpetual motion machine. It is more like an engine powered by fuel that comes to it through the ministry of Jesus Christ.

Creation involved a calculated risk. God knew that there was potential for trouble ahead. But the project must go forward. It had been agreed to, covenanted. The Creator would also be the Redeemer. He would represent the government of Heaven in all things pertaining to earth, "according to the eternal purpose which he purposed in Christ Jesus our Lord" (Eph. 3:11). There may have to be change orders, as they say in the construction industry. The plan may seem to go awry—plagued by detours and apparent delays. But nevertheless, the agreement will be carried out. There is the promise backed up by an oath: "Wherein God, willing more abundantly to shew unto the heirs of promise the immutability of his counsel, confirmed it by an oath" (Heb. 6:17). There is also the determination and commitment of the Mediator, who will "not fail nor be discouraged" (Isa. 42:4).

From the very outset mediation included this universal or cosmic dimension and also a second even more important aspect, the redemptive. It is important to understand that Jesus Christ administers both—the creative and redemptive. "Christ is the supreme agent or Mediator of God in creation and redemption."—*International Dictionary of the Bible,* p. 328.

In Creation Jesus demonstrated His divine power, His deity. Only God can create *ex nihilo,* that is, bringing something out of nothing. With God, word and deed are the same. Human creative genius involves merely rearranging preexistent matter. But when Jesus created the worlds, He was not dependent upon preexistent matter. He did not simply rearrange already existing molecules and atoms. Where there were no atomic particles, suddenly matter existed at His command. Furthermore, it is by His sustaining power that all things continue to exist.

There is a relationship between Creation and redemption. The power displayed in Creation and the prerogatives that belong to Jesus Christ as Creator are necessary to carry out the work of redemption. From the beginning, Creation and redemption are coupled together, and both are in the capable hands of the Mediator. "Their Redeemer is strong; the Lord of hosts is his name" (Jer. 50:34). Only someone equal to God could possibly accomplish the extensive mission that is the work of mediation. No one else has the power or the wisdom.

That brings us to another point. John calls the Mediator "the Word of God." In Jewish thought "the Word of God" came to mean much more than divinely originated intelligible sound. The prologue to the Gospel of John explains: "In the beginning was the Word, and the Word was with God, and the Word was God. The same was in the beginning with God" (John 1:1, 2). In the Gospel of John "one has turned into a quiet cathedral, where he is called upon to meditate upon the deep things of the Eternal Son of God—the Word made flesh! . . . John stresses the theme of Jesus as the Eternal Son, the *Logos* (Word). He existed with the Father before the foundation of the world, and he was the agent of God in the creation of the world."—*The Open Bible,* It Is Written Heritage Edition, p. 980. "All things were made by him; and without him was not any thing made that was made. In him was life; and the life was the light of men" (verses 3, 4).

"Christ, the Word, the only begotten of God, was one with the eternal Father—one in nature, in character, in purpose—the only being that could enter into all the counsels and purposes of God. 'His name shall be called Wonderful, Counselor, The mighty God, The everlasting Father, The Prince of Peace.' Isaiah 9:6. His 'goings forth have been from of old, from everlasting.' Micah 5:2."—*Patriarchs and Prophets,* p. 34.

"If Christ made all things, He existed before all things. . . . Christ was God essentially, and in the highest sense. He was with God from all eternity, God over all, blessed forevermore. . . . There are light and glory in the truth that Christ was one with the Father before the foundation of the world was laid. This is the light shining in a dark place, making it resplendent with divine, original glory. This truth, infinitely mysterious in itself, explains other mysterious and otherwise unexplainable truths, while it is enshrined in light, unapproachable and incomprehensible."—Ellen G. White, in *Review and Herald*, April 5, 1906, p. 8, quoted in *Questions on Doctrines*, p. 642.

Some Bible writers saw in Jesus Christ God's thought and wisdom personified. We find a most striking passage in the book of Proverbs. It is Wisdom who speaks. "The Lord possessed me in the beginning of his way, before his works of old. I was set up from everlasting, from the beginning, or ever the earth was. When there were no depths, I was brought forth; when there were no fountains abounding with water. . . . When he prepared the heavens, I was there. . . . Then I was by him, as one brought up with him: and I was daily his delight, rejoicing always before him" (Prov. 8:22-30).

Redemption's plan sprang from deep within God's heart. No one else could even announce it. At first it was known only to the Godhead. Even the angels remained ignorant of it. The apostles called it a mystery, *the* mystery. Is it not fitting that Jesus Christ, the mediator, had the privilege of making known that mystery? Appointed from the beginning, He shared fully in the universal development plan and brought it to fruition (through Creation and redemption). In His own person Jesus Christ articulates and epitomizes God's master plan for the earth and its inhabitants. The very thought of redemption comes to expression in Christ the eternal Word.

The ancient prophets spoke of the everlasting or eternal covenant. In modern language we talk about contracts and compacts. Nations speak in terms of treaties and agreements. The original covenant was made not between God and man, but in the Godhead. Holy, powerful hands were clasped. The agreement was made. God would not write off the earth as a bad debt, an unprofitable business—the sooner forgotten the better. Heaven would underwrite the venture and proceed with the creation of this new planet. And the God between, Jesus Christ, would be surety, the guarantor. "From everlasting He was the Mediator of the covenant."—*Evangelism,* p. 615.

Christ is therefore the supreme revealer of God. His mediatorial work involves revelation. Christianity is a mediated religion, a revealed religion. God takes the initiative. He shows Himself to us, not directly, but "through Jesus Christ our Lord." "No man hath seen God at any time; the only begotten Son, which is in the bosom of the Father, he hath declared him" (John 1:18).

"Before the entrance of evil there was peace and joy throughout the universe. . . . Christ the Word, the only-begotten of God, was one with the eternal Father—one in nature, in character, and in purpose—the only being in all the universe that could enter into all the counsels and purposes of God. By Christ the Father wrought in the creation of all heavenly beings."—*The Great Controversy,* p. 493.

"In speaking of His pre-existence, Christ carries the mind back through dateless ages. He assures us that there never was a time when He was not in close fellowship with the eternal God. He to whose voice the Jews were then listening had been with God as one brought up with Him."—Ellen G. White, in *Signs of the Times,* Aug. 29, 1900, in *Questions on Doctrine,* p. 644.

The Gospel of John records a number of "I AM" statements (see John 8:58; 10:14; 6:35). These sayings are of great significance. When God revealed Himself to Moses in the burning bush, He called Himself the "I AM." This divine name is probably built on a verb form that could be translated loosely as "he who is" or "the self-existent one." This name can refer only to Deity. The phrase is descriptive also of the limitless life that only God has. He is the source and fountain of life. Ellen White aptly puts it, "In Christ is life, original, unborrowed, underived."—*The Desire of Ages,* p. 530. By using the name "I AM," Jesus established His oneness with God in every respect.

The Mediator has great credibility. Who can question His credentials? He has the right, the authority, to redeem

Planet Earth. He is the only one who can speak confidently and on His own authority. His word takes precedence over the words of the prophets. Rabbis and religious teachers quoted the prophets as authoritative. But Jesus made His word supreme authority: "Ye have heard that it was said . . . : but I say unto you." He did not need to cite the great religious leaders of the past to support His claims. "For he taught them as one having authority, and not as the scribes" (Matt. 7:29). He revealed His Father, that is, He mediated the knowledge of His Father God not only by what He said and what He did but also in who He was. We feel the power of His words undiminished by the centuries in His reply to the woman at the well: "I that speak unto thee am he" (John 4:26).

The Gospel of John has seven of the "I AM" sayings. These major statements are connected with and illustrated by incidents or parables that could be called "Jesus' revelation of Himself in the Word." The "I AM" passages tell us who Jesus really is. They tell us what Jesus would have us to know about Himself, how He understood His own person and mission.

1. John 6. The theme of this chapter is the "bread of life," the "living bread" that came down from heaven. In verse 48, Jesus makes the bold declaration, "I am that bread of life." Notice how John links this revelation with a miracle. Jesus multiplied a lad's lunch of five loaves of bread and two fishes to meet the needs of five thousand men. The people were astonished and exclaimed, "This is of a truth that prophet that should come into the world" (verse 14). But Jesus wanted them to understand that He was more than a prophet or a miracle worker. He is the salvation for all men "come down from heaven." The miracle was not an end in itself. Jesus used it as a teaching device to bring the people to faith in Him, into direct contact with Him. Bread must be eaten in order to give life. Messiah is more than a great figure (or even the greatest) of history. Belief in Him is the only saving way to life.

2. John 7:1-8; 8. The Gospel writer here refers to the Feast

of Tabernacles, the national harvest festival. It was marked by impressive ceremonies, and its main themes were light and water. On the first night of the feast many oil lamps were lighted, illuminating the city of Jerusalem. The next morning the people paraded solemnly to the spring of Gihon, which flowed into the Pool of Siloam. The high priest drew water with a golden pitcher and poured it into a silver funnel or conduit. During Tabernacles great emphasis was placed on reading the Torah, the law of God. The Torah stood for wisdom. So we have in John 7 and 8 three key concepts: Jesus the teacher (He is Wisdom), Jesus the water of life, and Jesus the light of the world. He used the feast as an opportunity to proclaim Himself to be the wisdom of His Father, the water of life, and the light of the world.

3. John 9:1-10, 21. In this section of John's Gospel, Jesus tells the unbelieving Jews that He has been sent for our salvation. As the door (chap. 10:7), He provides the means of access to the heavenly Father. As the "good shepherd" (verse 11), He gives His life for the sheep and thus has the right, the authority, to be their supreme leader. The Sabbath day healing of the man born blind (chap. 9:1-4) calls attention to Jesus' mission of salvation. He gathers and shelters the sheep in His fold.

4. John 10:22-29. By the time of Jesus, the December festival of Hanukkah was associated with the dedication of the Temple and the miraculous kindling of fire on the altar of burnt offering in Nehemiah's time. During this festival Jesus openly declared, "I am the Son of God" (see chap. 10:36). "I and my Father are one," He said (verse 30). He is the sacred fire of sacrifice, the lamp of God, the true Shekinah, the visible manifestation of God's presence among us. He comes into the world as God's sanctifying agent, the new sanctuary, the altar consecrated by God Himself.

5. John 11:25. "I am the resurrection, and the life." At the raising of Lazarus Jesus uttered this "I AM" saying. Jesus defangs death, removes its sting, and ultimately destroys "the last enemy." The theme of John's Gospel is eternal life in Jesus the Son. Because He lives, physical death loses its

finality. The direct and personal communion and contact with Jesus through faith overcomes death. We are in touch with a life that is stronger than death.

6. John 14:6. "I am the way, the truth, and the life: no man cometh unto the Father, but by me." During the time of Israel's wilderness journey, Moses, with Yahweh before him, would locate a camping place. Jesus, the greater than Moses, has gone to prepare a place for His followers. In this most heartwarming and personal passage, He assures His followers: "I go before you, scouting the way, as it were, to prepare for you a camping place, a dwelling place. In my own person *I am* the way, reminiscent of the ladder that spans the distance between earth and heaven" (see chap. 1:51).

7. John 15:1-10. "I am the true vine, and my Father is the husbandman [vine dresser]." The symbol of the vine often appeared in Jewish literature. Israel pictured herself as a vine. Her prophets took up the symbolism. "Yet I planted you a choice vine" (Jer. 2:21, R.S.V.). Israel was a vine planted and cultivated by Yahweh. Later a great golden vine decorated the entrance to Herod's Temple. But in this saying Jesus emphasizes the new reality, "I am the *true* vine." His disciples are branches that receive nourishment from Him. They are not good if detached. Jesus stresses the absolute necessity of direct contact with Him. We are in Him, and He is in us.

So John has seven "I AM" sayings and seven works or signs. This is no accident. The number seven signifies perfection. The seven sayings reveal perfectly who Jesus is. They establish His relationship to the Father and explain His mission in the world. But in the final analysis we can understand all this only by the illumination of the Spirit, which He gives to believers.

The One who is commissioned to bring back the lost planet and to set things right in His Father's house (the universe) has all the qualifications to do the job. He has entered into the deepest secrets of the mind of Deity; nothing was kept back from the eternal Son. No plan of salvation could possibly predate Him, since He is before all things and there never was a time that He did not exist. He and His Father are one. There is complete identity here. He comes fresh from the throne, the inner circle, the *sanctum sanctorum.* The fullness of the Godhead is in Him bodily. "This Son is the radiance of his glory, just as the ray is the light of the sun. He is the exact impression of his being, just as the mark is the exact impression of the seal. It is he who sustains all things by the dynamic power of his word" (Heb. 1:3, Barclay).

There is a small pool of still, clear water in the cathedral at Chartres, France. The font is so situated that it reflects fully in every detail the huge ceiling with its impressive artwork—murals, frescoes, and exquisite design. We can safely say that all that God is, is mirrored accurately and completely in the person of Jesus Christ, our mediator.

Philo, the cultured Jew, thought of the *Logos,* God's Word, as His instrument of Creation—God's mind stamped on the universe, the tiller by which God steers the world, the bond that holds the world together, the high priest through whom God communicates with men.

I trust it is not too fanciful to say that at some point in eternity past the Almighty caused the angelic chorus to cease the hallelujahs. An announcement was about to be made. The master plan, long contemplated, was now ready for implementation. He (the Father) would share its essentials with the hosts of heaven. He would not tell all, but He would, at the least, disclose the broad outline. Cherubim and seraphim wait, voices hushed, for the Father to speak.

His powerful voice breaks the silence. "Thou art my Son," He says, motioning toward the preincarnate Jesus Christ (Ps. 2:7; see also Heb. 1:5). "Thy throne, O God, is for ever and ever: a sceptre of righteousness is the sceptre of thy kingdom. . . . Thou, Lord, in the beginning hast laid the foundation of the earth; and the heavens are the works of thine hands: they shall perish; but thou remainest. . . . Thou art the same, and thy years shall not fail" (Heb. 1:8-12). "Let all the angels of God worship him" (verse 6).

Although they cannot fully grasp God's great secret, their hearts are strangely warmed. Filled with adoration and praise, they strike their harps again and again and sing with all their might, "Thou art worthy, O Lord, to receive glory and honour and power: for thou hast created all things, and for thy pleasure they are and were created" (Rev. 4:11).

*Before the world was!* A master plan, a strategy was conceived *before the world was*—to be administered by One equal to God, One who is God, One who has a unique relationship and position within the Deity. As we meditate on this greatest of all mysteries, the mystery of godliness, our minds go back before time began. There were communion, musing, a planning session, and then the process began. Our thoughts leap forward, and we see the great vision. This relationship that existed before time began, that continues now while time runs, and that will endure when time shall be no more is revealed in Jesus Christ, the Mediator, our Saviour and Lord. It is only natural that we join the chorus: "Worthy is the Lamb that was slain to receive power, and riches, and wisdom, and strength, and honour, and glory, and blessing. . . . Blessing, and honour, and glory, and power, be unto him that sitteth upon the throne, and unto the Lamb for ever and ever" (chap. 5:12, 13).

# *OPERATION RESCUE*

*The cosmic drama of redemption takes on the nature of a sea rescue operation.*

*"Picture a little outboard foundering in the swirling currents of a whirlpool. Picture the men aboard sick with exhaustion and the gas and the oars long gone. The boat is not yet lost down the funnel, but it veers closer and closer. A rescue cutter sights the boat, but cannot reach it or make fast to it for the sea is too rough and the men too weak to catch or hold a line. So the strongest man aboard the cutter takes a coiled line over his shoulder and dives into the waves. He swims to the little boat, makes one end of the line fast to a cleat, and swims the other end of the line back to the cutter, climbs aboard and makes it fast to a winch. There is still much to be done, to be sure, but in fact the boat has been saved."—Edmund A. Steimle, ed.,* Renewal in the Pulpit, *p. 13.*

Chapter 2

# BETWEEN TWO WORLDS

"Though earth was struck off from the continent of Heaven and alienated from its communion, Jesus has connected it again with the sphere of glory."—*Sons and Daughters of God,* p. 244.

Geologists conjecture that all the great continents now separated by oceans were once a great solid land mass. But, they further speculate, the continent Pangea split apart, separating into our present continents. They see evidence of this continental drift in the jigsaw puzzle outline of some of the continents, which, it seems, would almost fit if they could be brought together.

I'm not sufficiently informed to make a judgment here. But I do know that earth was at one time a part of the continent of heaven, something like a crown colony. The same will of God that governed heaven also governed earth. Instead of a great gulf between earth and heaven, there was perfect communication. Whereas scientists conjecture that the once-solid land mass of a single continent floated apart into separate continents, we have the Bible's word that our first parents' sin separated earth from heaven.

To change the analogy, the fallout of Adam and Eve's sin like deadly atomic radiation has polluted the atmosphere and has made it necessary for God to quarantine the earth. All nature has become involved and suffers. The ground is cursed, although once it brought forth superabundantly. Extremes in climate mar the planet in rebellion—the same planet where once the atmosphere was conducive to health and comfort. There are harmful bacteria and viruses. There are thistles and thorns, briars and brambles. And, yes, there is death. It is a gloomy picture, and it all came about because of one person's sin. "Wherefore, as by one man sin entered into the world, and death by sin; and so death passed upon all men, for that all have sinned" (Rom. 5:12). Sin, then, is a terrible disease. Unfortunately, humanity is the carrier.

I have often wondered why the sin of our first parents caused such a change in the natural world. Why such a violent reaction, even in the atmosphere? "Through man's disobedience a change was wrought in nature itself."—*Testimonies,* vol. 8, p. 256. It could well be because Adam was the first federal head of the human race. He had sovereignty under God over earth. God told him to be fruitful, multiply, and exercise dominion. Adam was God's steward. All was placed in his hands. Heaven instructed him to dress and keep the Garden, to preserve the creation. God trusted Adam and put him in charge. Adam's sin, therefore, is of no little consequence. The colony of heaven became a rebel camp—all because of Adam and Eve's sin. "For . . . by man came death. . . . For . . . in Adam all die" (1 Cor. 15:21, 22).

Back for a moment to the spaceship illustration. A terrible epidemic has swept through the craft, and all the passengers on board are suffering from the same disease. None escape, and there is no known cure. The malady must be contained and limited to Planet Earth. It must be dealt with here where it began. But the great problem is that out of contact with the Life-giver, earth becomes a dying planet.

The situation seems hopeless. But all is not lost. "Behold, the Lord's hand is not shortened, that it cannot save; neither his ear heavy, that it cannot hear: but your iniquities have separated between you and your God, and your sins have hid his face from you, that he will not hear" (Isa. 59:1, 2). The lost planet doesn't stand a ghost of a chance. It carries within it the seeds of death. No wonder Paul pictured the whole creation as suffering under bondage. "For we know that the whole creation groaneth and travaileth in pain together until now" (Rom. 8:22).

This little spaceship, out of orbit and doomed to certain

destruction, is like the lost sheep in Christ's parable—it does not know it is lost, and it cannot save itself. Unless someone appears on the scene, some good shepherd, it will surely perish. Again, this is a terribly gloomy picture. But this is the way the Bible paints it—just as it is, no false hopes, no vain promises, just stark realism. As the old preacher in "God's Trombones" states it: "Blacker than a thousand midnights down in a cypress swamp."

The Mediator has, as we say, His work cut out for Him. We need a breaththrough, an opening in the impenetrable cloud cover that thickly shrouds the planet. Isaiah makes it even more somber. "For, behold, the darkness shall cover the earth, and gross darkness the people" (Isa. 60:2). The Mediator's challenge? To break through and reestablish communication.

I remember an overnight plane trip I took from Boston to Paris. The nearer we got to Europe, the denser the cloud cover became, until when we were over Paris, there was zero visibility. The foggy cloud cover reached down to the ground. But our plane was equipped with the most sophisticated instrumentation, the kind of radar that can pierce almost any fog, no matter how dense. We passengers saw nothing but the heavy mist. Even after landing, planes on the runway and buildings looked ghostly and eerie. Powerful electric lights feebly shone like little candles. We actually could not see the terminal until we were right next to it. In fact, we approached the gate with a great deal of difficulty. We all worried that some other less-equipped vehicle would plow into us. At De Gaulle Airport I was to change planes for Bern, Switzerland, but nothing could take off in that fog. It was a miracle that we landed safely.

Our Mediator faced a similar challenge. How could He break through? He assumed human nature. He came in contact with humanity through incarnation. He established solidarity with mankind, complete identity. His was and is no make-believe humanity. One of the first great heresies of the Christian church insisted that Jesus did not really become a human being; He only seemed to be one. For divinity to become humanity is something totally unique, a genuine breakthrough.

We speak about a breakthrough in science or a breakthrough in international relations. Breakthrough signifies something unprecedented, something never achieved before. Barriers are broken. Walls are pierced. A road is opened. New possibilities, new opportunities, a whole new set of circumstances arise. Jesus Christ made humanity His own—bone of His bone and flesh of His flesh. As someone has put it, God *gave* Him to us. Jesus is not a loan, but a gift. Somewhere on His descent to humanity He passed the point of no return, just as that plane did on my trip to Paris.

Of necessity God had to quarantine and contain sin on this planet. It must be limited, for it jeopardized the whole universe. The dying planet must be put in isolation. Thus Christ could not successfully and completely carry out His mediatorial ministry in heaven. He must risk the journey to earth. He must deal with the problem there. Jesus' parable of the lost sheep is really about a lost planet, the only one that went astray. It did not know it was lost. It couldn't save itself. Some good shepherd must go out into the desert, take the risk, and make the sacrifice to bring it back.

"By the lost sheep Christ represents not only the individual sinner but the one world that has apostatized and has been ruined by sin. This world is but an atom in the vast dominions over which God presides, yet this little fallen world—the one lost sheep—is more precious in His sight than are the ninety and nine that went not astray from the fold. Christ, the loved Commander in the heavenly courts, stooped from His high estate, laid aside the glory that He had with the Father, in order to save the one lost world. For this He left the sinless worlds on high, the ninety and nine that loved Him, and came to this earth, to be 'wounded for our transgressions' and 'bruised for our iniquities' (Isa. 53:5). God gave Himself in His Son that He might have the joy of receiving back the sheep that was lost."—*Christ's Object Lessons,* pp. 190, 191.

Jesus has effected a breakthrough. Communication has been restored. He has taken up His position between heaven and earth. He descended and ascended, thus making the connection and completing the circuit. Heaven and earth now can talk to each other again.

A good many years ago preachers fondly told the story of a young Army officer—perhaps during the Civil War—who used his own body to connect two hot wires. As I remember it, the enemy had separated two battalions. Survival depended on communication. But there were no wireless radios in those days. A young officer volunteered to carry a line through no-man's-land, hoping to reach the isolated battalion. It was an almost impossible task, yet he almost made it to the trenches when his line ran out. Someone threw him another line over the ramparts. Having no time to splice it, he grasped one line in his right hand and the other in his left. The current flowed through him. Communication was restored. (I can't tell you how the story ended, but this is the way I remember it.)

You will recall Jacob's fearful journey. Driven by a guilty conscience, he fled from home and happened upon a certain place where he tarried all night because the sun had set. "And he took of the stones of that place, and put them for his pillows, and lay down in that place to sleep. And he dreamed, and behold a ladder set up on the earth, and the top of it reached to heaven: and behold the angels of God ascending and descending on it" (Gen. 28:11, 12). Jacob heard a voice from the top of the ladder. It assured him that the God of his fathers was with him. Upon awakening the next morning, Jacob recognized the place as the house of God and the gate of heaven.

More than two millenniums later the words of Jesus illuminated Jacob's experience and gave it deep spiritual meaning. "And he saith unto him, Verily, verily, I say unto you, Hereafter ye shall see heaven open, and the angels of God ascending and descending upon the Son of man" (John 1:51). Jesus is the ladder. He reaches from earth to heaven and heaven to earth. He Himself effected a breakthrough in communications. He grasps the throne of heaven with one hand, and with His other arm he encircles the globe. In His humanity He touches earth, and through His divinity He reaches to high heaven. The Incarnation, Christ's becoming truly human, says to us on this doomed planet, "You need not be cut off. You need not be isolated." Though the gloom still enshrouds the earth and the effects of sin's fallout still bear baleful fruit, the connection has been made that will never be broken.

Think of the Incarnation as breakthrough and the cross as follow-through. "And I, if I be lifted up from the earth, will draw all men unto me" (chap. 12:32). The Incarnation established His solidarity with the human family. He became our brother. The cross has become the great magnet, the attraction that draws all unto Him. Like the strong swimmer that we referred to previously, Jesus attaches the line firmly to Planet Earth, and then He secures it to heaven. The connection cannot be broken.

Mediation involves rescue. It involves confrontation with the powers that held the whole race hostage. Satan was determined to maintain his foothold. He thought he could erect barriers that would effectively keep the planet under his dominion. "No man can enter into a strong man's house, and spoil his goods, except he will first bind the strong man; and then he will spoil his house" (Mark 3:27). Jesus crashed the sin barrier, did battle with the hijacker, and broke the stranglehold. It was a fearful struggle, but "on that cross he discarded the cosmic powers and authorities like a garment; he made a public spectacle of them and led them as captives in his triumphal procession" (Col. 2:15, N.E.B.).

"The cross of Calvary challenges, and will finally vanquish, every earthly and hellish power. In the cross all influence centers, and from it all influence goes forth. It is the great center of attraction, for on it Christ gave up His life for the human race."—*Sons and Daughters of God,* p. 242.

The cross was not "an unfortunate accident," as someone put it, Jesus being mangled on the wheels of history. It was part of God's master strategy. Jesus the mediator would storm the gates, attack the enemy, and destroy him. Jesus came to win back His lost creation, to establish contact—communication—between two worlds. No, He was not mangled on the wheels of history, but He took hold of history. He took hold of the world. He took hold of two worlds. Our Mediator entered the stream of history, rode its rage, ruled its flood, and bent its course.

The cross was a mighty deed. At great personal cost to God, the broken wires were spliced at Calvary. The connection was made. The cross was not some tragic Friday afternoon mistake caused by a mix-up at Jerusalem city hall. God was in charge all the time. He was in Christ putting Himself wholly into the saving act, and that saving act, that heroic deed, reestablished vital communication between earth and heaven.

We must not think of our Mediator as a helpless victim only. He triumphed as victor. He came on a search-and-destroy mission. "For this purpose the Son of God was manifested, that he might destroy the works of the devil" (1 John 3:8). "That through death he might destroy him that had the power of death, that is, the devil; and deliver them who through fear of death were all their lifetime subject to bondage" (Heb. 2:14, 15). He could say as the great military leader, "We have met the enemy and they are ours." "He [Christ] died on the cross to give the death-stroke to Satan, and to take away the sin of every believing soul."—Ellen G. White manuscript 61, 1903, in *Questions on Doctrine,* p. 679.

"What right had Christ to take the captives out of the enemy's hands? The right of having made a sacrifice that satisfies the principles of justice by which the kingdom of heaven is governed. He came to this earth as the Redeemer of the lost race, to conquer the wily foe, and, by His steadfast allegiance to right, to save all who accept Him as their Saviour. On the cross of Calvary He paid the redemption price of the race. And thus He gained the right to take the captives from the grasp of the great deceiver."—Ellen G. White, in *Signs of the Times,* Sept. 30, 1903, in *Questions on Doctrine,* p. 679.

"The victory gained at His death on Calvary broke forever the accusing power of Satan over the universe."—Ellen G. White manuscript 50, 1900, in *Questions on Doctrine,* p. 679.

"He [Christ] planted His cross midway between heaven and earth, that He might wrestle with and overcome the powers of darkness. He gave His life for the life of sinners, and Satan, the prince of the world, was cast out."—Ellen G. White manuscript 44, 1901, in *Questions on Doctrine,* pp. 679, 680.

"When with the cross before Him, the Saviour uttered the sublime prediction, 'Now shall the prince of this world be cast out. And I, if I be lifted up, shall draw all men unto me,' He saw that the great apostate, who had been expelled from heaven, was the central power in the earth. Looking for Satan's throne, He found it set up where God's should have been. He saw all men worshiping the apostate, who inspired them with rebellion. The inhabitants of this world had prostrated themselves at Satan's feet. Christ declared, Where stands Satan's throne, there shall stand My cross, the instrument of humiliation and suffering."—Ellen G. White manuscript 165, 1899, in *Questions on Doctrine,* p. 680.

The Mediator overcame the space and time barrier, the logistical problem of distance. He overcame the principalities and powers that would prevent Him from bringing the lost planet back into harmony with the continent of heaven. Now a new set of circumstances exists. The kingdom of God has really been inaugurated. There are new possibilities. Heaven's gates are open. Angels of God ascend and descend the shining ladder. With the aid of the Holy Spirit we can tune in on heaven's wavelength. No longer can the enemy jam the signals.

The future is so firmly in the hands of the Mediator that Paul could affirm that the last days had already begun. Satan's death knell has sounded. He is indeed cast down. He fights now only a war of attrition. There is no possibility of his activity ever threatening the universe of God anymore. Christians can speak as if the consummation had already taken place. They already sit with Christ in heavenly places.

The outcome of the cosmic conflict is no longer in question. In just a matter of time "the long-continued alienation of the celestial and terrestrial spheres from each other will cease, and all estrangement from God in these regions . . . is to be set aside."—Walter Scott, in Herbert Lockyer, *All the Doctrines of the Bible,* p. 192. "The *Incarnation* divides time; the *Crucifixion* eternity."—Lockyer, *loc. cit.* The work of the Mediator spans time and joins the eternities.

Those who lived through the days of World War II remember D-Day and V-Day. A contemporary theologian has used this analogy to illustrate the relationship between the first and second comings of Christ. "D-Day was but the prelude to V-Day, the Day of Christ, the Parousia [Second Coming], the day of final victory of God in Christ. It is the conviction that though the campaign may drag on and V-Day, the day of final glory may still be out of sight, D-Day is over and the powers of evil have received a blow from which they can never recover."—Archibald M. Hunter, *Interpreting Paul's Gospel,* p. 127.

Another analogy comes to mind, the *visitation* and the *invasion.* It is based on Hebrews 9:28. "So Christ was once offered to bear the sins of many; and unto them that look for him shall he appear the second time without sin unto salvation." Notice the sequence. First, the visitation—Bethlehem, Nazareth, Capernaum, Jerusalem—the days of His earthly sojourn: without fanfare or ostentation; no trumpets to herald His coming. Second, the invasion—to finish what He began in the visitation. Now come the power, the glory, and the trumpet blast. The visitation centers upon the manger and the cross. The invasion focuses on the crown and the throne.

*Introduction to Chapter 3*

# *MEANWHILE, BACK ON THE SPACESHIP*

*The passengers on the ill-fated spacecraft are really hostages. They have absolutely no way of escape, but they are joined in the solidarity of death. They are all on a journey to utter extinction. And to add to the gloom, everyone on board suffers from a fatal malady, an incurable disease. And what is worse, they don't know they have it. Yet every one of them is a carrier.*

*From time to time some of their fellow passengers through some mysterious illumination are made aware of the true situation. They claim to have a message from outer space. But hardly anyone believes them. In fact, when the other passengers can no longer ignore those who claim illumination, they simply do away with them—though later they build monuments to these very people whom they martyred.*

*At times some of the passengers feel like shouting, "Stop, I want to get off!" Impossible. There is nowhere to go. The spaceship cannot land anywhere. They are quarantined, and no port will have them. Then as they sit around in despair, someone recalls that strange Passenger and says, "He promised deliverance. Something about His blood shed for a ransom. He said He was the door. Maybe there is a way out. Maybe He is the way out! He seemed so calm and self-assured when He said, 'I am the way.' Yes, I believe Him. Let's go tell everyone on board. We know now. He is for real!"*

Chapter 3

# BETWEEN GOD AND MAN

Seventh-day Adventists have come to look on salvation history as the "great controversy." Although this may seem unique in theological circles today, the idea or concept did not originate with us. It has deep Biblical roots. There was war in heaven. Michael and his angels fought against the dragon and his angels. Michael, of course, prevailed, and expelled Satan, who was previously known as Lucifer (the morning star).

The warfare continues here. The whole Bible, it seems, is oriented toward the idea of a cosmic drama that is not limited to one tribe, nation, or single people. The whole world is involved. The apostle Paul speaks about a struggle "against principalities, against powers, against the rulers of the darkness of this world, against spiritual wickedness in high places" (Eph. 6:12). Gustav Aulen in his influential book *Christus Victor* develops this motif or theme as used by Bible writers and the early Church Fathers.

Again, when we look at the Bible through a wide-angle lens, taking the overview, we can see the conflict moving from stage to stage. New Testament teaching groups itself around a single point, redemption. The theme is clear: All men are held in bondage under the powers of evil—the flesh, sin, death. To the Bible writers these are not abstractions, but active forces. The inspired writers also speak of another order of powers of evil—demons, principalities. Satan stands at the head of these demonic powers, whom God has permitted to have dominion for a time. Irenaeus, one of the early Christian fathers, said that Christ came down to destroy sin, overcome death, and give life to humanity. Aulen calls this the dramatic view. It focuses on supernatural conflict and divine victory. Christ fights and triumphs over the evil tyrants that hold us in bondage. And in Christ God reconciles the world to Himself. Aulen uses such phrases as "a drama of salvation" and "a cosmic drama." Someone must come to destroy these powers that have subjected mankind to bondage. Someone must break the stranglehold. So Heaven takes the offensive. As the military men say: "The best defense is a good offense." The Mediator is the one designated from all eternity to come to the hostile planet to rescue the hostages.

We should consider another point. The hostages have become rebels. They have joined the archenemy. So the Mediator's work is even more difficult. He has the strength and power to overcome the enemy. But He must do so in such a way as not to destroy the rebel hostages. He must do more than make a way for them to escape. He must persuade them of their peril and of His love for them. They must come to trust Him. The situation calls for a Mediator, skillful, trustworthy, capable, all-powerful, and all-accomplishing.

A Biblical illustration comes to mind. Lot let himself get separated from Abraham. He flirted with danger. Finally he fell into captivity. He was utterly powerless and helpless. A hapless prey. Abraham heard about Lot's predicament, armed a band of strong men, and led them to the rescue. By sheer might and power—military strength—he overcame the enemy, rescued his nephew, and set him free.

So it is with sinners. Ours is the most abject and cruel slavery. We do not believe in original sin in its classical form, that is, Adam's sin makes all men culpable and guilty. What Adam passed on to his posterity was not his own guilt but his own fallen nature, which predisposes us to sin and makes us all easy prey, almost willing accomplices. "For all have sinned, and come short of the glory of God" (Rom. 3:23). All the descendants of Adam become entangled in his fate because they inevitably repeat his mistake—they choose to join the great archenemy. We are all individually responsible for our own sin.

We cannot get through a study such as this without considering some theological words and concepts. The first is *sin,* the breaking of God's law (see 1 John 3:4). Sin is disobedience to God, departure from His idea of righteousness. Furthermore, sin fractures relationships.

"It was Augustine and then Calvin who used the concept of alienation to emphasize that the problem of sin or evil was not just theological but relational—a breach of man's relationship with God entailing a breach of all other relationships. The alienation of evil is theological, between God and man; sociological, between man and other men; psychological, between man and himself; and ecological, between man and nature."—Os Guinness, *The Dust of Death,* pp. 35, 36.

The apostle James wrote about the sequence: "Then when lust hath conceived, it bringeth forth sin: and sin, when it is finished, bringeth forth death" (James 1:15). The determination to go one's own way, to do one's own thing, leads to sin, and that leads ultimately to death. "For the wages of sin is death" (Rom. 6:23).

The second word we need to look at, then, is *death.* In its deepest theological sense it means separation from God. He is the source of life, and to be separated from Him is to die.

So the Biblical viewpoint is that all humanity is not simply in bondage but in rebellion. Paul reminded the Ephesian Christians that they were at one time "dead in trespasses and sins" (Eph. 2:1). He also wanted them to know that during this period of their existence they "walked according to the course of this world, according to the prince of the power of the air, the spirit that now worketh in the children of disobedience: among whom also we all had our conversation in times past in the lusts of our flesh, fulfilling the desires of the flesh and of the mind; and were by nature the children of wrath, even as others" (verses 2, 3). The situation calls for a Mediator.

Remember, in the earliest sense of the word, the

Mediator is one who goes out from where He is. He goes out of His way to become a negotiator, broker, intermediary, go-between. He takes His place not only between two worlds, heaven and earth, but between God and man.

We find an illustration in the parable of the good Samaritan. The Scripture says that the Samaritan "came where he was: and when he saw him, he had compassion on him, and went to him, and bound up his wounds, pouring in oil and wine, and set him on his own beast, and brought him to an inn, and took care of him" (Luke 10:33, 34). It was our great need, our terrible predicament, our hopeless estate, that drew Christ out of the ivory palaces and into this world of woe. He had compassion on us, came where we were, put His hands on us, and took care of us.

The Mediator, then, must touch humanity. He is already firmly rooted in Deity. Now He must establish unquestioned solidarity with the human family. This, of course, was done through the Incarnation, when He became real, live humanity—flesh and blood. This was God's way of touching humanity without destroying humanity. God could not come down to live unveiled among us. We have groveled in the dark cellar of sin too long to stand the brightness of even an angel's countenance, let alone unmediated Deity.

Another illustration comes to mind. I was privileged to visit a mission station in Africa where we got our lights and power by generator. Electricity, therefore, was very precious. It had to be rationed. At ten o'clock sharp all lights went out. However, I had noticed high-tension wires running adjacent to our property. So I asked the principal of the school why we couldn't tap the tremendous power in those great high-tension wires. "That's a good question," he answered. "In order to utilize the tremendous voltage in those wires, we would need a transformer. Transformers are very, very expensive, and in addition to that, we would need permission from the government to do so."

Then I thought, The great power of the Godhead is communicated to humanity through a transformer, Jesus Christ, who steps down the voltage but not the quality of divine energy. The Incarnation made it possible for Deity to touch humanity without consuming us. Later on I asked an engineer friend what would happen if I were to plug my wife's toaster into all that power which flows through the high-tension wires. "Simple," he said. "It would just burn up." Then I thought of the words of Jeremiah: "It is of the Lord's mercies that we are not consumed, because his compassions fail not. They are new every morning: great is thy faithfulness" (Lam. 3:22, 23).

Through the Incarnation Jesus Christ established an unbreakable solidarity with humanity. He can now serve as substitute and surety for the human family. He can do things in our stead, on our behalf. He is one of us.

*Substitution* is another one of those great theological words that we need to study. The experience of Abraham and Isaac on Mount Moriah offers a classic example of substitution (see Genesis 22). Abraham, with heavy heart, led his son up the mountain and then proceeded to follow God's instructions to the ultimate. As he raised his hand to slay Isaac, the angel voice stopped him. When he looked to the thicket, he spied a ram caught there, which he used as a substitute. Although Isaac typifies Christ, the ram also is a type of our Saviour, who became a substitute for humanity. The great London preacher C. H. Spurgeon used to say that he could summarize his theology in four words, "He died for me."

During the Civil War a draftee could pay a substitute to enter the Army in his place. We have all heard stories that have come from those years, such as the man who was seen weeping in a cemetery. "A relative?" a fellow mourner asked. "Father? Mother? Friend?"

Each time the man shook his head. "No, none of these. When I was conscripted, this man went to the Army in my place. He caught the bullet that should have been mine. This man died for me."

But the hostages need more. They need actual rescue. This brings us to another Biblical word, *redemption.* You will find it used in both the Old and New Testaments. One of the words translated by "redeem" has as its root meaning "to release by a ransom." It refers to the price paid for freeing a captive. First Peter 1:18 uses the word in this way: "Forasmuch as ye know that ye were not redeemed with corruptible things, as silver and gold, from your vain conversation received by tradition from your fathers."

Another word translated as "redeem" meant to buy up something in the marketplace. Young in his analytical concordance renders it "to acquire out of the forum." Our Redeemer went into the marketplace to buy us, and He set us free from our captivity.

An Old Testament word *paraq,* translated as "redeem" and "deliver," means to break off, to tear away, hence to rescue. It denotes a violent action. The Redeemer wrests His prey from the enemy.

There is another Old Testament word that implies not only the idea of redemption and ransom but also adds the dimension of avengement. This word brings into view the office of the *goel*—the kinsman, deliverer, redeemer, husband, and avenger. Prophets applied this particular term to the time when Christ would return to avenge His chosen people. As Kinsman-Redeemer He will avenge the saints of all wrongs suffered at the hands of the world, death, and the devil. "The great gospel work in the book of Ruth is that of redeeming. This relates to the nearest of kin, who had the right to acquire the former possessions of his friend by paying the ransom price. In Boaz, the kinsman of Elimelech, 'a mighty man of wealth,' we have another beautiful type of the redemption provided by Christ. The name Boaz means 'ability.' What a fitting title to apply to Christ. As the God-man, He is our Kinsman-Redeemer. He has not only the right but the ability to save, even to the uttermost, all who come unto God by Him. The power to redeem fallen man was not vested in the angels, for they were not 'nigh of kin.' Christ did not take on Him the nature of angels, but the seed of Abraham (Heb. 2:14-16). Therefore He is not ashamed to call us brethren (verse 11). The patriarch Job recognized Christ as the near Kinsman, the

'Goel,' when he looked forward to a life beyond the tomb. 'I know that my redeemer [near-Kinsman] liveth, and that he shall stand at the latter day upon the earth' (Job 19:25)."—*Our Firm Foundation,* vol. 1, p. 356.

In Old Testament times the kinsman-redeemer performed a number of functions, all of which typified the work of Christ, our mediator. A person who was sold in captivity could be redeemed by one of his brothers (see Lev. 25:25). As our elder Brother, Christ has the right to redeem us (see Heb. 2:14-18).

Very early in Biblical history the figure of the *goel,* or redeemer, emerged. Under the ancient law the *goel* had three rights. 1. He could buy back the property rights of an Israelite who had been forced to sell himself into bondage through poverty. Adam bargained away the inheritance of the human family, but Christ in assuming humanity became the Goel-Redeemer who saves the race from being disinherited eternally. 2. If the Israelites fell in bondage to a foreigner, the *goel* was responsible for his ransom. It is the Saviour's blood that is the price for our redemption. 3. In the very earliest times the *goel* avenged the death of his slain kinsman as a point of honor. The Mediator came to destroy him who has "the power of death, that is, the devil," thus avenging his brethren who have been destroyed by the murderer (Heb. 2:14).

There is yet another word that we need to consider—*reconciliation.* It could be well the grandest word of all. Reconciliation means restoration to divine favor, bringing things and persons back to God. In every instance the Bible talks about man being reconciled to God. It never speaks about God being reconciled to man. God has been wounded. We have always been the offenders. Our sin has separated us from God, and Scripture pictures us as being at enmity with God. (See Isa. 59:1, 2; Rom. 8:7.) Someone has to make reconciliation between God and man. Furthermore, we must not think of Christ's death as satisfying an angry God, appeasing Him and awakening sympathy in His heart for lost humanity. It is always God who works in Christ to reconcile the world unto Himself. (See 2 Cor. 5:19.)

"God never 'gave' in order to 'love.' He gave because He loved. The cross was not the cause of God's love, but the effect of it. God, then, is *not* reconciled to sinners, for He has ever loved them, and has never been estranged from them. Not He, but *we*, needed the reconciliation. He has never been alienated from His sinful, guilty creatures, but they were and are strangers to Him, and need to be made *at one* with Him. Christ is the blessed Reconciler, reconciling enemies to God (Rom. 5:10, margin; Col. 1:20-22; 2 Cor. 5:18-20). He is the Daysman betwixt us (Job 9:35)."—Lockyer, *All the Doctrines of the Bible*, p. 191.

Because of all of His activity, His victory, and His complete identification with humanity, Jesus Christ is able to save to the uttermost. He can reconcile and forgive and pardon and cleanse and ransom and redeem. His blood becomes efficacious and powerful.

But the clearest illustration of these profound spiritual truths is found in the ancient sanctuary and its services. Seventh-day Adventists are right in emphasizing this great teaching device. The way of God was taught here (Ps. 77:13)—how He deals with sin, removes and destroys the accursed thing. We find it all there in that microcosm of salvation. We would do well to study it with deep interest and close attention. The spiritually enlightened Israelite clearly understood, as he brought his sacrifices to the tabernacle, the principle of substitution.

The priestly book of Leviticus describes offerings of all kinds. It prescribes how sacrifices were to be made, what the worshipers were to do, and what the priest was to do. Very early in the book the worshiper is instructed to "put his hand upon the head of the burnt offering; and it shall be accepted for him to make atonement for him" (Lev. 1:4). The offerer identified himself with the offering. By laying his hands upon the sacrifice, he transferred his guilt to the Lamb in exchange for the innocence of the sacrifice. The Saviour in effect exchanged places with the repentant sinner. He "was treated as we deserve, that we might be treated as He deserves" *(The Desire of Ages,* p. 25).

It is interesting to note that when a priest sinned, or when all the people sinned, the blood of the victim was carried into the sanctuary. In both instances the priest was instructed to "dip his finger in the blood, and sprinkle of the blood seven times before the Lord, before the vail of the sanctuary. And the priest shall put some of the blood upon the horns of the altar of sweet incense before the Lord, which is in the tabernacle of the congregation" (chap. 4:6, 7; see also verses 17, 18). In the instance of the individual sinner, the blood was sprinkled on the horns of the altar of burnt offering and poured out at the base of the altar (verse 30). But when the whole congregation of Israel sinned or when the priest as the representative of the congregation sinned, a further step was taken. The blood was carried into the sanctuary itself, placed on the horns of the altar of incense, which stood before the veil, and sprinkled seven times. (See Lev. 4:3-7, 13-17.)

Israel was a congregation, a people, a community. Yahweh dealt with them as a corporate body. The daily sacrifices and personal offerings were constant reminders of sin. The Israelite who brought them in faith was assured of being incorporated into the covenant people. Evening and morning sacrifices and their personal response to the claims of Yahweh made it possible for them to claim the promise "I, even I, am he that blotteth out thy transgressions for mine own sake, and will not remember thy sins" (Isa. 43:25). As the representative of redeemed humanity our great High Priest takes upon Him our sins. "The Lord hath laid on him the iniquity of us all" (chap. 53:6).

On the Day of Atonement all that had been done before throughout the year was repeated. "Then shall he kill the goat of the sin offering, that is for the people, and bring his blood within the vail, and do with that blood as he did with the blood of the bullock, and sprinkle it upon the mercy seat, and before the mercy seat: and he shall make an atonement for the holy place, because of the uncleanness of the children of Israel, and because of their transgressions in all their sins: and so shall he do for the tabernacle of the congregation, that remaineth among them in the midst of their uncleanness. . . . And he shall sprinkle of the blood upon it with his finger seven times, and cleanse it, and hallow it from the uncleanness of the children of Israel" (Lev. 16:15-19).

The actual atonement took place in the sanctuary. That is where sin is dealt with. In some mysterious way that we do not understand, the heavenly places also need cleansing and hallowing from the uncleanness of God's people. If we are to take the words of Scripture seriously, then we shall also have to say that the holy place, the tabernacle of the congregation, and the altar need reconciling. (See verse 20.)

Early Seventh-day Adventist preachers and Bible teachers were quite correct in insisting that the atonement in its wider aspect was not complete until something happened within the sanctuary on the annual Day of Atonement. It was then and only then, after the sins had been separated from the camp, that sin had been adequately dealt with.

There is much more here than we can cover in this little volume. Suffice it to say, however, that the Mediator became one of us, took our place, acted on our behalf, and has the power to pardon, forgive, and actually eradicate sin. It is not simply a matter of sin being forgotten over the millenniums. It is a matter of providing a full and complete remedy.

D. L. Moody used to say, "It was the blood that did it." The estrangement and hostility are overcome—the Mediator makes peace. He joins in His own person divinity and humanity, and He makes this effective through His sacrifice on Calvary and His continuing ministry in the heavenly sanctuary. He stands between God and mankind and reconciles us to God. He opens up the possibility of fellowship. He provides access to God. Repentant sinners may come boldly to the throne of grace and know that God hears them. Rebels need not remain rebels. God offers a general amnesty for all who will throw down the weapons of their warfare and accept the terms of surrender so graciously offered them by Christ the victor.

There is a finished work, and there is a continuing work. It involves past, present, and future. "Who delivered us from so great a death, and doth deliver: in whom we trust that he will yet deliver us" (2 Cor. 1:10). The Mediator is strong to deliver from sin's penalty, its power, and ultimately from its presence. Now the travelers on this biosphere have a remedy for that fatal malady. They have a representative who is their substitute and surety at the very power center of the universe. He appears in the presence of God on their behalf. (See Heb. 9:24.)

*Introduction to Chapter 4*

# *STORY OF THE RICH MAN AND HIS POOR FRIENDS*

*(Unfinished Scenario)*

*The scenario goes like this: There was a fabulously rich man, quite eccentric. He had everything that one could wish for or even dream of—yachts and villas. He was the head of several multinational companies. He was confidant of statesmen and presidents. Business and financial journals had a good time guessing how wealthy he really was.*

*But as I said, he was eccentric. Wealthy man that he was, he had six very poor friends. It seems that they lived near his main residence. No one could understand why he took up so much time with them. They spent evening after evening in his game room. He treated them as equals.*

*Then one day he called them into his library. His attorney was there. It was about his will. It was all drawn up now, and he wanted to let his friends know what they could expect. "We've had some good times together," he said, "and some bad. And I think a lot of all of you. That's why I am letting you in on the terms of my will. You are included. In fact, this home where we have spent so many evenings together in the game room will be yours. But there is one contingency. You must live here, the six of you, under this one roof for one year without speaking a cross word. You must live here in absolute peace—no quarreling—for the entire year. After that, the mansion will be yours, no strings attached."*

Chapter 4

# BETWEEN MAN AND MAN

One of humanity's basic needs is community. We are social beings. A person growing up in complete isolation could hardly be expected to become a fully functioning human being. The search for unity with other human beings is perennial, never-ending. Witness the many seminars and workshops on personal development. The phenomenon has become a veritable movement. "Human potential" counselors and lecturers crisscross the continent, developing their own constituencies and followings. It has become a real growth industry. People want to reach out and touch other people. They want to belong. They want to be needed, and they need other significant human beings in their lives. But alas!

Sad evidence of the Fall shows up in our inability to achieve genuine community. The human race is divided, fractured, alienated—characterized by enmity, hostility, and antisocial behavior. In the best of communities, families, and churches, human relations are tenuous at best. Try as we may, it is well-nigh impossible to bridge these separating gaps. An entire race victimized by its own passions and prejudices is sin's legacy. The situation calls for a Mediator—someone to bring us together, to create community.

The Mediator is the supreme peacemaker. Isaiah's prophecy names Him so. "For unto us a child is born, unto us a son is given: and the government shall be upon his shoulder: and his name shall be called Wonderful, Counsellor, The mighty God, The everlasting Father, The Prince of

Peace" (Isa. 9:6). His mission is to create peace. Paul says, "He is our peace" (Eph. 2:14). Christ clears away the hostility that exists between God and us.

How does He accomplish this reconciliation? "By the work and merit of Jesus Christ, who . . . put aside everything that would interpose between man and God's pardoning love."—*Sons and Daughters of God,* p. 239. So we might say that Jesus clears the way. Ellen White puts it this way: "He has cast up a glorious highway."—*Ibid.,* p. 230. The way is opened. As Dr. Jack Provonsha puts it in the title of his recent book, you *can* go home again.

Since the Mediator has come, an entirely different situation, a whole new set of circumstances, prevails. The guilty pair driven from their Eden home now have access. All their sons and daughters may enter in through open gates. It bears repeating: the cross is the instrument of peace. "Without the cross, man could have no union with the Father. On it depends our every hope. From it shines the light of the Saviour's love; and when at the foot of the cross the sinner looks up to the One who died to save him, he may rejoice with fulness of joy; for his sins are pardoned. Kneeling in faith at the cross, he has reached the highest place to which man can attain."—*Ibid.,* p. 222.

This is the meaning of the torn veil. At the time of the Crucifixion, the huge curtain that separated the Most Holy Place from the view of the high priest, who represented the congregation, was ripped from top to bottom. By an act of God aliens, strangers, foreigners, those who were afar off, "are made nigh by the blood of Christ" (Eph. 2:13). "The mercy seat, upon which the glory of God rested in the holiest of all, is opened to all who accept Christ as the propitiation for sin, and through its medium, they are brought into fellowship with God. The veil is rent, the partition walls broken down, the handwriting of ordinances cancelled. By virtue of His blood the enmity is abolished."—*Ibid.,* p. 228.

The New Testament writers exult in this great reality that became the dominant theme of apostolic preaching.

"Therefore being justified by faith, we have peace with God through our Lord Jesus Christ: by whom also we have access by faith into this grace wherein we stand, and rejoice in hope of the glory of God" (Rom. 5:1, 2). The cross is pivotal. And it is the power of the cross that slays the enmity. (See Eph. 2:16.)

Paul used the imagery and thought forms of the first century in his attempt to make plain what really had taken place. He pictured principalities and powers standing in the way, challenging the Lord of life. At the head of this confederacy of evil stands Satan. He breathes out threatenings and uses every weapon at his disposal to thwart God's plans and purposes. But he is overcome, thoroughly defeated, by that cross. The Mediator abolished in His flesh the enmity and hostility. (See verse 15.) Zacharias, father of John the Baptist, saw this clearly and described the mission of the Christ child. "To give knowledge of salvation unto his people by the remission of their sins, through the tender mercy of our God; whereby the dayspring from on high hath visited us, to give light to them that sit in darkness and in the shadow of death, to guide our feet into the way of peace" (Luke 1:77-79). He came to give light and peace.

But the cross as a fact of history is not sufficient. Christ must make this peace experiential. He must take His place between each person and his neighbor. He must inaugurate a reign of peace on earth. As a very young person I learned a verse that goes like this: "Though Jesus Christ a thousand times in Bethlehem be born, if He is not reborn in thee, thy soul is still forlorn." This peace, which is such a beautiful sentiment, must take up residence in flesh and blood—men and women, boys and girls—or Heaven's strategy is thwarted. Jesus, therefore, becomes the God between us and our fellows. He becomes, as someone put it, "the third Person in all human relationships." Remember, inherent in the concept of the Mediator is the thought of equidistance. Jesus stands between us—close enough to touch each of us. "For he is our peace, who hath made both one, and hath broken down the middle wall of partition between us" (Eph.

2:14). Jesus stoops to involve Himself in human relations as a human being among humanity.

Sin has left as its legacy division and hostility. D. L. Moody used to say, "Sin leaped into the world full grown, as the first boy born became a murderer." P. T. Forsyth said it graphically: "The disease is mortal. And, moreover, what is in question is a diseased world. It is a society that is sick to death, and not a stray soul. We have to deal with a radical evil in human nature, and spiritual wickedness in deep places."—*Positive Preaching and the Modern Mind,* p. 234.

Six millenniums of history provide more than ample evidence that ours is a troubled planet, war-weary and blood-soaked. No mere palliative will meet the situation—like taking aspirin for heart disease or putting a band-aid on cancer. God has provided strong medicine. "Through His death, He provided a way whereby man may break with Satan, return to his allegiance to God, and through faith in the Redeemer obtain pardon."—*Sons and Daughters of God,* p. 230.

And His legacy is peace. "Peace I leave with you, my peace I give unto you: not as the world giveth, give I unto you. Let not your heart be troubled, neither let it be afraid" (John 14:27). "These things I have spoken unto you, that in me ye might have peace. In the world ye shall have tribulation: but be of good cheer; I have overcome the world" (chap. 16:33).

Peace as the Hebrews understood it was not simply a cessation of hostilities or the absence of open fighting. Peace in the Biblical sense means goodwill. It has strong, positive connotations. This peace has an active and possessive quality about it. The Hebrew word is *shalom.* It was used as a greeting, and it meant, "May everything go well with your health, family relations, and neighbor relations." In this sense, peace suggested the adjustment of all that has to do with life, health, and happiness. All debts were paid. One's enemies were under control. No threatening clouds darkened the horizon. As they say, blue skies would be there all the way. The righteous, believing Hebrew could think of no greater good than *shalom.*

Yet this condition does not exist for most peoples. Peace, as the Bible speaks of it, does not issue from the natural human heart. "Because the carnal mind is enmity against God: for it is not subject to the law of God, neither indeed can be" (Rom. 8:7). Jesus cataloged the iniquity that resides in the human heart. "For from within, out of the heart of men, proceed evil thoughts, adulteries, fornications, murders, thefts, covetousness, wickedness, deceit, lasciviousness, an evil eye, blasphemy, pride, foolishness: all these evil things come from within, and defile the man" (Mark 7:21-23).

We belong to an endangered species. Our own bloody hands jeopardized our future. We're both the hunter and the hunted. Our innate tendency to violence makes the race prone to self-destruct. The Mediator, however, hastens to our rescue, to save us from destroying ourselves. He creates peace. He creates a new order of humanity. "Having abolished in his flesh the enmity, even the law of commandments contained in ordinances; for to make in himself of twain one new man, so making peace" (Eph. 2:15).

Paul was speaking here about the creation of a new community. Jew and Gentile are brought together and fused into a new humanity—the people of God. "But as many as received him, to them gave he power to become the sons of God, even to them that believe on his name: which were born, not of blood, nor of the will of the flesh, nor of the will of man, but of God" (John 1:12, 13). Jesus taught His disciples to pray, "Thy kingdom come. Thy will be done in earth, as it is in heaven" (Matt. 6:10). This new community, this new Israel of God, is really a colony of heaven. The rule of God is effective here. Obedience to God and loyalty to Jesus Christ mark the lives of the saints. The church of the living God is an outpost, a sign that God *does* dwell with humanity. The church is indeed and in fact His fortress that He holds in a revolted world. Church members are to shine as lights "in the midst of a crooked and perverse nation" (Phil. 2:15). They drive with their headlights on—illuminating the darkness and pointing the way to a better life, life in Jesus Christ.

The church is a colony of heaven. It is also a laboratory where God is performing human experiments, experiments that amaze angels and demons alike. The Mediator's plan is to gather into one all things and all persons. He takes these strangers and foreigners and makes them fellow citizens, part of His household. He incorporates them into a building where He Himself is the chief cornerstone. This building takes on the properties of a living organism, growing and developing. "In whom ye also are builded together for an habitation of God through the Spirit" (Eph. 2:22). The community of the redeemed is very important in the economy of heaven. Here all humanity are to have an illustration and demonstration of true community. It is possible. It can be a reality. God expects it and demands it. The peace of Christ is active, dynamic. It is a positive force.

Our powerful Priest-King issues this peace from His mediatorial throne. He calls it "great peace" (Ps. 119:165; Isa. 54:13). "It is great because it is able to fortify our hearts and minds (Phil. 4:7). The word here means 'garrison,' which speaks of a fortified place where soldiers are quartered. Peace as a sentinel guards us, as a sentry guards a palace."—Lockyer, *All the Doctrines of the Bible,* p. 216.

The old adage has it that the proof of the pudding is in the eating. So the proof of Christianity is in the church. It is a contradiction of terms that strife should mar the community of peace. God has made adequate provision that Christ's followers be models of genuine peace. They can attain this desired state because Jesus is in their midst. "For where two or three are gathered together in my name, there am I in the midst of them" (Matt. 18:20). Early in the book of Revelation John paints an impressive picture. He heard a great trumpet voice speaking. It is the Alpha and Omega. As John turned to see the Person behind the voice, he viewed instead seven golden lampstands that represented the churches. And then he recognized, "In the midst of the seven candlesticks one like unto the Son of man, clothed with a garment down to the foot, and girt about the paps with a golden girdle" (Rev. 1:13). John saw the risen Christ who walks among the churches. He stands between believers. He mediates to them, without restriction, His peace.

It is surprising to observe how often this theme is repeated throughout the entire Bible. The wicked have no peace. They are like the troubled sea that casts up muck and mire. There is no peace, saith the Lord, to the wicked. On the other hand, the righteous have the fruit of peace. They have great peace. It surrounds them and their children. (See Isa. 26:3; 48:18; 54:13; Ps. 119:165.) "God's peace is no trickling stream, but boundless as a mighty, surging river, and like a swelling river, it broadens and deepens and fills up."—*Ibid.*

At the very outset we said that the work of the Mediator is to help parties work together harmoniously toward common or mutual goals when they cannot do so on their own. He brings erstwhile rebels together in a community of service where growth and development and fulfillment take place. "They helped every one his neighbour" (Isa. 41:6). The apostle Paul went right to the heart of the matter. He gave us a formula, good instructions to "the new man, which is renewed in knowledge after the image of him that created him: where there is neither Greek nor Jew, circumcision nor uncircumcision, Barbarian, Scythian, bond nor free: but Christ is all, and in all. Put on therefore, as the elect of God, holy and beloved, bowels of mercies, kindness, humbleness of mind, meekness, longsuffering; forbearing one another, and forgiving one another, if any man have a quarrel against any: even as Christ forgave you, so also do ye" (Col. 3:10-13).

The great principles of salvation's plan must be worked out in the crucible of human experience. Christ's work has concrete results. The church is not homogeneous. It is always heterogeneous. The scope of redemption is international and interracial, including "every nation, and kindred, and tongue, and people" (Rev. 14:6). The worldwide church of the living God is the true and authentic United Nations. There is more pointed, spiritual instruction that modern Christians must take seriously: "Endeavouring to keep the unity of the Spirit in the bond of peace. There is one body, and one Spirit, even as ye are called in one hope of your calling; one Lord, one faith, one baptism, one God and Father of all, who is above all, and through all, and in you all" (Eph. 4:3-6).

The unity that exists in the Godhead is the model. It is to be reproduced on earth in the church. We know that Satan is active, sowing all kinds of discord among believers. He would alienate Christians from one another. He would like nothing better than to bring in party strife and pride and prejudice. We need to remember that Christ's shed blood has already secured peace for us. This is an unalterable, unchangeable fact. "Comfort ye, comfort ye my people, saith your God. Speak ye comfortably to Jerusalem, and cry unto her, that her warfare is accomplished, that her iniquity is pardoned: for she hath received of the Lord's hand double for all her sins" (Isa. 40:1, 2). The prophet closest to us in time has said: "The powers of darkness stand a poor chance against believers who love one another as Christ has loved them, who refuse to create alienation and strife, who stand together, who are kind, courteous, and tenderhearted, cherishing the faith that works by love and purifies the soul. We must have the Spirit of Christ, or we are none of His."—*Sons and Daughters of God,* p. 286.

If we will turn to Him as the disciples did in their extremity when their little boat was threatened by angry waves, He will exercise His kingly power and speak peace. He still commands the elements. He is the master of earth and skies. As a result of His sacrifice, there will be within time and history a community made up of human beings who have made Him supreme, the Lord of their lives. These people are fiercely loyal to Jesus Christ. They love Him, obey Him, and keep His commandments. The peace of God rules in their hearts. They are called into one body. Their thanks and praise to Him know no bounds. (See Col. 3:15.)

So there is worship and praise in the community, because Jesus Christ, our high priest, ministers in both spheres—the inner sanctuary above and the outer court below. "The most characteristic function of Christ in

Christian worship, then, is understood to be mediation: He mediates human worship to God, and He mediates salvation from God to humanity."—Geoffrey Wainwright, *Doxology*, p. 66.

*Introduction to Chapter 5*

# *THE LAST JUDGMENT IS AT HAND*

*"For a long time and with almost inconceivable patience God has kept to Himself in the face of the ravings of the godless; now He finally rises up in flaming anger. He summons all Jews and Gentiles to assemble before His throne, in order to expose 'all ungodliness and unrighteousness of men who suppress the truth by unrighteousness' and to see to it that they harvest what they have sown. He now proves Himself to be 'judge over the world.' The moan, 'How long, O Lord, how long . . . ?' and the desperate or furious cry for the appearance of the God of vengeance are stilled. At last God is waiting no longer, but has decided to exercise His royal prerogative. Earlier acts of judgment concerned individual men, Israel, or at the most some of the nations; this time God is judging the whole earth and every man together. While there are many judges handling the law and using power within the jurisdictions entrusted to them, God is now judging the universe, including the judges, petty and supreme. He has jealously kept the final judgment for Himself. No one can cope with all the unrighteousness and injustice of the world and master it except God. . . .*

*"Those who have heard of God and have had to transmit what they have heard can in no way get around God's vehement anger against evil. God's anger is the temperature of His love. Only God's own vehemence against all sin is able to check injustice on earth. . . . No Supreme Court of the future will have superior jurisdiction or be able to question what takes place now and today in this court."—Marcus Barth,* Justification, *pp. 25, 26.*

Chapter 5

# BETWEEN US AND JUDGMENT

The Biblical writers often used the phrase "the wrath of God." Paul refers to the wrath of God many times in his letters. Sometimes in Scripture His wrath is spoken of as being great (see Zech. 7:12). It "is revealed from heaven against all ungodliness and unrighteousness of men, who hold the truth in unrighteousness" (Rom. 1:18). The impenitent are pictured as treasuring up "wrath against the day of wrath and revelation of the righteous judgment of God; who will render to every man according to his deeds" (chap. 2:5, 6). Those who are contentious and disobedient can expect only "indignation and wrath" (verse 8). This wrath is caused by apostasy (2 Chron. 34:21, 25); sin (Joshua 22:20); forsaking the Lord (2 Kings 23:13); fellowship with evil (2 Chron. 19:2); idolatry (Ps. 78:58, 59); profaning the Sabbath (Neh. 13:18); and unbelief (Ps. 78:19-21). We cannot escape the awful reality of God's wrath. The unregenerate are called "children of wrath" (Eph. 2:3). Indeed, the Biblical writers looked into the future and saw a great day of wrath, a day of judgment, when all—nations and individuals—who are in rebellion will drink of the wrath of God.

These are fearful words. Modern theology seeks to avoid them. But the wrath of God still remains a reality. The wrath of God is His attitude toward sin and evil rather than the intemperate outburst of an uncontrollable character. "By 'the wrath' Paul means God's holy displeasure at sin. It is the eternal divine reaction against evil without which God would not be the moral Governor of the world. Paul thinks of it as both present and future. It is that divine aversion to evil and sin which, though active in the present time, will not reach its climax till the Judgment."—Archibald M. Hunter, *The Gospel According to St Paul,* p. 71.

It is a good and loving God who reacts against evil with wrath. Even decent human beings become indignant over injustice and cruelty. A lack of anger in the face of cruelty really exhibits a lack of love or a failure to care for others. The total reality of the wrath of God is known, however, only as we go to Gethsemane and Calvary, where we see our Saviour suffering the wrath that should have been ours. God is consistent, unchanging. His attitude toward sin is the same today as it was on that day when His Son suffered the full penalty for our sin.

God's attitude toward sin makes the judgment inevitable. He must deal with the sin problem. He must stem the tide of evil that threatens to engulf the universe. Not only must He stem the tide, but He must turn it back, cut it off at its source, destroy the spring.

The Father alone knows the deadly nature of sin. It is called the "mystery of iniquity," an active principle that if unchecked would destroy the very foundations of God's government. His sovereignty over earth, now challenged, will actually be lost if something is not done. At the proper time God rises to meet the challenge. The Mediator's work proceeds according to plan. Although it is all directed from the sanctuary, from the throne room, it is worked out in the arena of human history. The mystery of iniquity is met and answered by the mystery of godliness. "God was manifest in the flesh, justified in the Spirit, seen of angels, preached unto the Gentiles, believed on in the world, received up into glory" (1 Tim. 3:16).

It is interesting to note that the judgment or courtroom theme is dominant throughout Scripture, especially in the Old Testament, where the setting is that of a law court. Israel was first ruled by judges who were to judge righteously, to dispense justice with equity. "The judge is addressed as the helper or redeemer of the party that considers itself wronged. The mere fact that a case is taken up by a court in session (in the gate, in the royal palace or in the sanctuary) can be called justification or righting the wrong."—Barth, *Justification,* p. 19. Elsewhere in the Old Testament we encounter the idea of a great and final litigation between God and His people or between God and the world. Scripture writers develop the idea more and more until they picture the great judgment of the last times. The Old Testament court proceeding was therefore a conflict between two parties that ended with victory for that party whom the judge pronounced to be in the right. "Thus the Old Testament itself knows a history of judgment imagery in which annihilation and establishment, curse and blessing follow each other far and near, somehow mysteriously bound together."—*Ibid.,* p. 18.

The apostle Paul expanded the Old Testament idea into his great doctrine of justification by faith. "At this point one sees plainly that Paul regards history as God's trial with the world which will come to an end only in the last judgment and will result solely in the victory or defeat of one or the other party. . . . In this struggle for vindication the issue is who is truthful and constant and who is the liar."—Ernst Käsemann, *Commentary on Romans,* p. 81.

The overarching theme, then, that joins both Old and New Testament revelation and human history is the God of Heaven's summoning nations and individuals to court/judgment. All are accountable to Him. He is judge. His law is the standard of judgment. As in the Old Testament court scene, evidence is introduced, witnesses are called, the matter is investigated, and a decision is rendered.

In this judgment all are condemned because "all have sinned, and come short of the glory of God" (Rom. 3:23). "The terrible predicament of the nations and of God's chosen people can be changed only by the intervention in God's court of a reliable, bold, and skillful advocate. Legal aid and assistance are required."—Barth, *Justification,* p. 35. The situation calls for a Mediator, someone to stand in the breach. "But now God surprises the court by sending His Son. 'But when the time was fulfilled, God sent his Son. . . . In view of the inability of the law, which was weak because of the flesh, God sent His Son in the likeness of sinful flesh.' Jesus Christ was sent to be an advocate (in biblical language a 'witness') for the accused. 'God appointed Him as an intercessor,' which means as a mediator, a pleader, a defense attorney, or, in the Swiss-German language a *Fürsprech* (speaker-for-us)."—*Ibid.,* p. 37.

So, then, "we have an advocate with the Father, Jesus Christ the righteous" (1 John 2:1). He provides legal aid of the highest order. The One whom God sends takes His stand entirely on the side of the accused. He builds solidarity between Himself and them. "Wherefore in all things it behoved him to be made like unto his brethren, that he might be a merciful and faithful high priest in things pertaining to God, to make reconciliation for the sins of the people. For in that he himself hath suffered being tempted, he is able to succour them that are tempted" (Heb. 2:17, 18). He represents us in the judgment.

The book of Daniel portrays the judgment in the setting of influential kingdoms. The nations are pictured as bloodthirsty beasts, predators. They struggle for power and supremacy. They challenge God's sovereignty. They oppose His truth and persecute His saints. The rebellion progresses until the little horn power takes the stage. He speaks "great words against the most High," wears out "the saints of the most High," and thinks "to change times and laws" (Dan. 7:25). His career lasts for 1,260 years ("a time and times and the dividing of time" [verse 25]). "But the judgment shall sit, and they shall take away his dominion, to consume and to destroy it unto the end. And the kingdom and dominion, and the greatness of the kingdom under the whole heaven, shall be given to the people of the saints of the most High, whose kingdom is an everlasting kingdom, and all dominions shall serve and obey him" (verses 26, 27).

As Daniel saw this trend in human history, truth apparently always on the scaffold and wrong seemingly occupying the throne, he wondered, How long? A heavenly being echoed his question. The answer comes in Daniel

8:14: "Unto two thousand and three hundred days; then shall the sanctuary be cleansed." This cleansing of the sanctuary also vindicates the ways of God, setting things right in the universe and establishing His righteous government forever.

The Biblical idea of judgment centers upon a throne (see Ps. 103:19; Jer. 17:12). God's throne is founded in righteousness, but there is a rival throne (see Ps. 94:20; Isa. 14:13). The great controversy involves a clash of rival thrones struggling for the supremacy. That's why the key thought in Daniel's prophecy is dominion. Who will ultimately prevail? What throne will emerge victorious? Will it be the throne of God, or will it be the throne of the usurper who would make himself God (the "mystery of iniquity")?

The Almighty bears long. He is patient. But finally He brings the matter into court. If God is to maintain His credibility as moral governor of the universe, He must act. He must set things straight. In mercy He reveals the time frame. Read very carefully Daniel 7-9. The heavenly court sits in judgment (1) after the little horn power has done its work and (2) before the second coming of Christ and the establishment of the kingdom of glory. This judgment takes place during "the days of these kings." It is a settling of accounts, a universal audit. Every detail is scrutinized. Nothing is swept under the rug.

The judgment described has three major dimensions: (1) Satan is unmasked and condemned, (2) God's name and character are completely vindicated, and (3) the saints of God are cleared and given irrevocable citizenship in the kingdom of heaven.

Something did happen in heaven in 1844. The throne on wheels moved beyond the veil into the Holy of Holies. Then one like a Son of man, a human figure, one who identifies with us, was ushered into this same chamber. He now stands between us and the wrath of God—the judgment. He holds all power in His hands—the power of life, immortality. He can represent us better than we can represent ourselves, and He confers irrevocable citizenship upon those who trust in Him. The judgment is totally in His hands. He combines in His person the offices of prophet, priest, and king, and in His ministry the legislative, judicial, and executive powers of government. He is Michael, who stands up on behalf of His people (Dan. 12:1). Judgment is pronounced in favor of the saints. It is given *for* the saints (see chap. 7:21, 22, R.S.V. and N.E.B.). The sanctuary is restored to its rightful state (see chap. 8:14, R.S.V.), and the holy place emerges victorious (see verse 14, N.E.B.).

It seems only natural that the sanctuary should be the place of judgment. The throne of God is there. The sanctuary, therefore, is the control center of the universe. Here Satan began his accusations against God's government. Since the ultimate decisions are made here, the sin problem must ultimately be resolved here. The book of Hebrews addresses this issue. "The priests entered regularly into the outer room to carry on their ministry. But only the high priest entered the inner room, and that only once a year, and never without blood." "It was necessary, then, for the copies of the heavenly things to be purified with these sacrifices, but the heavenly things themselves with better sacrifices than these. For Christ did not enter a man-made sanctuary that was only a copy of the true one; he entered heaven itself, now to appear for us in God's presence. Nor did he enter heaven to offer himself again and again, the way the high priest enters the Most Holy Place every year with blood that is not his own. Then Christ would have had to suffer many times since the creation of the world. But now he has appeared once for all at the end of the ages to do away with sin by the sacrifice of himself" (Heb. 9:6, 7, 23-26, N.I.V.).

Our Mediator knows how to deal with sin and has pledged Himself to do so. He is the sin bearer (see verse 28). Through His mediatorial ministry our sins are carried away. They are laid on Him, and He bears them (Isa. 53:6; 1 Peter 2:24). But our Mediator provides for more than the removal of a legal barrier. He provides for cleansing—actual and complete removal of sin.

Once again the earthly sanctuary is the model. It demonstrated God's way of dealing with sin. "Thy way, O God, is in the sanctuary" (Ps. 77:13). Its ritual called for the total destruction of the fat of the sacrificial animal (Ps. 37:20). The purpose of the altar fire was to consume utterly. Nothing was left. The contaminating substance was annihilated. Whatever defiles in the universe, therefore, must be eliminated.

We have a modern-day illustration of this reality. Scientists are hard put to know what to do with nuclear waste, a terribly deadly contaminant that retains its potency for up to fifteen thousand years. The accumulation of nuclear waste threatens the future of life on earth. Scientists must find a way to get rid of it without polluting the earth.

Jesus entered fully and completely into the human experience. He put Himself at risk. Now, because He is victorious, without sin, wholly harmless, undefiled, He can take upon Himself our sins and remain undefiled. He carries our sins into the sanctuary, into the very presence of the holy God, and there God deals with them. He has the right, the prerogative, and the power to do this.

The Day of Atonement ritual in ancient Israel portrayed the final resolution of the sin problem. The elaborate and intricate ceremony was meaningful in every respect: the vigorous scrubbing and washing required of the priests, the scrupulous attention to detail and to the sequence of ritual events, the solemnity attached to everything involved, the total absorption of the worshipers with expectation, hope, complete attention, and waiting. Every nerve was stretched, for the consequences were enormous and far-reaching. There was a finality about the entire ceremony. The activities of this high, holy day were significant for eternity. Even modern secular Jews recognize something special about Yom Kippur—the Day of Atonement.

Seventh-day Adventists are right in insisting that sin must be dealt with. An entire universe has been affected by the defection of Satan, Adam, and Adam's race. But the Mediator makes thorough work. By His plan and through

His ministry, the curse is removed. It is thoroughly extirpated. So the prophet predicted, "Affliction shall not rise up the second time" (Nahum 1:9). Sin and sinners cannot and will not coexist with God and the righteous throughout eternity. Sin will not be simply contained somewhere in the universe. There will be absolutely no coexistence. No trace will be left.

As the ancient high priest stood before the mercy seat in the presence of the holy Shekinah and sprinkled the blood seven times, so Jesus stands before His Father. He offers His blood, which satisfies justice entirely. Atonement, therefore, involves the taking away of sins. The very record and remembrance of sin must be expunged.

The key sentence occurs in Leviticus 16:16: "And he shall make an atonement for the holy place, because of the uncleanness of the children of Israel, and because of their transgressions in all their sins: and so shall he do for the tabernacle of the congregation, that remaineth among them in the midst of their uncleanness."

"The blood has removed the sins of the people. In Hebrews 9-10 this ritual of the Day of the Atonement is applied to Jesus. As a high priest He passes through a celestial outer court into the heavenly Holy of Holies where God is present (9:11, 24); He does not do this once a year but once for all (9:7, 12); He does not bring the blood of bulls (He has no sin of His own: 7:26, 27) or the blood of goats but His own blood—He is the spotless victim who has offered Himself at the end of the ages (9:12-14), and His sacrifice is consummated in heaven . . . where He is now seated at the right hand of God (10:12). Indeed, His blood continues to purify (9:14), offering encouragement: . . . 'We have confidence to enter the sanctuary by the blood of Jesus' (10:19). Since according to the Law things are cleansed with blood 'and without the shedding of blood there is no forgiveness of sins' (9:22), believers are sanctified and purified through this sacrifice of Christ (10:10), and sin is annulled (10:17, 18). There is no doubt that the sacrifice of Christ on the once-for-all Christian Day of Atonement described in Hebrews is more an expiation than a propitiation."—*The Anchor Bible, The Epistles of John,* vol. 30, pp. 220, 221. In this case expiation means an activity that is essentially intended to remove sin—taking it out of the way.

Jesus is our advocate as well as our intercessor. He is the attorney for the defense. Satan's ancient legal role in relation to sinners was portrayed as that of accuser before the judgment seat of God (see Job 1:6-12; Zech. 3:1-3). Jesus turns the tables. Those prosecuted in the divine judgment are those who refuse to believe in Jesus, while those defended successfully are those who believe in Him. Daniel and the other prophets saw the truth of God cast to the ground and the saints of God persecuted and "rubbed out." Christ, the victor, goes to the Father, casting Satan out of the heavenly court (see John 16:7, 10, 11; 12:31; Rev. 12:10). "This means that believers now have someone who defends them before God instead of accusing them."—*Ibid.,* p. 217. The heavenly court provides expert legal aid. "We have an advocate with the Father, Jesus Christ the righteous; and he is the expiation for our sins, and not for ours only but also for the sins of the whole world" (1 John 2:1, 2, R.S.V.). This is Day of Atonement language, and according to a Talmudic tradition: "On the Day of Atonement Satan is deprived of every power to accuse Israel."

Jesus is the central figure in the heavenly tribunal. His own words make this very clear. "For the Father judgeth no man, but hath committed all judgment unto the Son. . . . And hath given him authority to execute judgment also, because he is the Son of man" (John 5:22-27).

"Christ has been made our Judge. The Father is not the Judge. The angels are not. He who took humanity upon Himself, and in this world lived a perfect life, is to judge us. He only can be our Judge. Will you remember this, brethren? . . . Christ took humanity that He might be our Judge."—*Testimonies,* vol. 9, p. 185. "Christ Himself will decide who are worthy to dwell with the family of heaven."—*Christ's Object Lessons,* p. 74. "Because He has tasted the very dregs of human affliction and temptation, and understands the frailties and sins of men; because in our behalf He has victoriously withstood the temptations of Satan, and will deal justly and tenderly with the souls that His own blood has been poured out to save—because of this, the Son of man is appointed to execute the judgment."—*The Desire of Ages,* p. 210.

So the judgment is absolutely necessary—to answer all the arguments. Satan's charges are answered! God's throne is made secure! The saints are exonerated and cleared and assured citizenship in the kingdom of God! "In every legal procedure it is not only the accused who is on trial. The accuser is on trial; the court system, the law, justice . . . are on trial; and in a special way even the judge is on trial."—Barth, *Justification,* p. 64.

God's righteous judgment, His treatment of individuals in His court, moves all creation to break out into a doxology. "Great and marvellous are thy works, Lord God Almighty; just and true are thy ways, thou King of saints. Who shall not fear thee, O Lord, and glorify thy name? for thou only art holy: for all nations shall come and worship before thee; for thy judgments are made manifest" (Rev. 15:3, 4). "God's judging is in the end edification, building up; that in setting things *right* He has set them *upright* and saved His whole creation."—*Ibid.,* p. 77.

Seventh-day Adventists have a sobering word for this generation—a word of warning, even of stern rebuke. It is a relevant word that was recorded in the first century. The twentieth century is the time for its playback. "And I saw another angel fly in the midst of heaven, having the everlasting gospel to preach unto them that dwell on the earth, and to every nation, and kindred, and tongue, and people, saying with a loud voice, Fear God, and give glory to him; for the hour of his judgment is come: and worship him that made heaven, and earth, and the sea, and the fountains of waters" (chap. 14:6, 7). As officers of the court we must serve notice on the world that the hour of God's judgment has come.

Paul preached to the Athenians about an appointed day in which God "will judge the world in righteousness by that man whom he hath ordained" (Acts 17:31). In his defense before King Felix, Paul "reasoned of righteousness, temperance, and judgment to come" (chap. 24:25). The parable of Matthew 22 talks about the great wedding, the marriage, and the feast. There were three calls. The first call was largely ignored. "They would not come" (verse 3). The second call was met with hostility. Not only did the people make light of the king's invitation, but they "took his servants, and entreated them spitefully, and slew them" (verse 6). But the king persisted. He was determined that he would have guests at the marriage feast, so he sent out the call to "as many as ye shall find" (verse 9). "So those servants went out into the highways, and gathered together all as many as they found, both bad and good: and the wedding was furnished with guests" (verse 10).

But this was not the end of the matter. The king had invited them to a formal affair. As we would say today, black tie and evening dress. It should not have surprised anyone that the king came in to examine the guests. After all, he had prepared the feast. Furthermore, he had also provided wedding garments for all who needed and desired them. It was not enough simply to come for the big supper. Preparation was required. The proper attire was expected. "And when the king came in to see the guests, he saw there a man which had not on a wedding garment: and he saith unto him, Friend, how camest thou in hither not having a wedding garment? And he was speechless" (verses 11, 12).

The inference of the parable is quite clear. All who would go into the feast must wear the wedding garment. All who would go into the feast must bear the inspection of the king. The improperly clad guest was speechless. He had no excuse, because the king had graciously provided a wedding garment. The consequences were serious. "Then said the king to the servants, Bind him hand and foot, and take him away, and cast him into outer darkness; there shall be weeping and gnashing of teeth. For many are called, but few are chosen" (verses 13, 14).

So we have it from Jesus' own lips—there will be an investigation of persons and a deciding of cases, an investigative judgment, if you please.

Some of our friends take issue with the doctrine of an investigative judgment. They call it double jeopardy, trying a person twice for the same crime. But we must remember that salvation is not a paid-up insurance policy. "But he that shall endure unto the end, the same shall be saved" (chap. 24:13). Ernst Käsemann, the New Testament scholar, is right when he says, "Assurance of salvation is not salvation secured."—*Commentary on Romans,* p. 238. "The justification of the ungodly can come only from the Judge. . . . The righteousness of God . . . is the central concept in Paul's theology. . . . This righteousness . . . manifests itself in a saving way in God's love for the creature. But it does that in the judgment. . . . Only the judged who have been set in their proper place are saved."—*Ibid.,* p. 320.

The mediatorial ministry of Jesus Christ moves from the prophetic (that is, the revelation of the character of God, "the light of the knowledge of the glory of God in the face of Jesus" [2 Cor. 4:6]), to the priestly (where the man who represents God to us becomes the man who represents us to God because "he ever liveth to make intercession for them" [Heb. 7:25]), and finally to the judicial (where the priest becomes the judge-advocate, "who shall judge the quick and the dead at his appearing and his kingdom" [2 Tim. 4:1]). Salvation is all of Jesus Christ. And all of salvation is mediated. "Since Christ was not only installed as their virtual or potential representative but actually as the fully empowered manager of their case, now that Jesus Christ is judging them their case cannot possibly be lost altogether."—Barth, *Justification,* p. 78.

We have an important, universal word to deliver, and we cannot hold back. We stand squarely in the prophetic tradition. We simply speak what we have seen and heard. Our testimony is that of the prophets and of our Lord Himself. Is it not love that motivates and compels us to warn everyone on the spacecraft that "we must all appear before the judgment seat of Christ; that every one may receive the things done in his body, according to that he hath done, whether it be good or bad" (2 Cor. 5:10)?

*Introduction to Chapter 6*

# *SPACE-AGE PARABLE— JOURNEY'S END*

*For the travelers on Spaceship Earth it has been a terrible odyssey. Six millenniums. One tragedy after another. Rebellion. Insurrection. Bloodshed. Pestilence. Plague. Death. Since the original defection by passenger number one, it has been a tragic series of bad incidences.*

*For a long time the craft was enshrouded by an impenetrable gloom, a thick fog. Then came breakthrough. The mysterious Visitor, the Man from Wayout, quietly came aboard. He becomes the Second Passenger. Whereas the first passenger brought on the plague, He brings the cure. The Second Passenger makes the difference. Ever since His arrival, stabs of light have knifed through the heavy cloud cover. Passengers in the darkness have seen light, and the glimmers of that light have brought them hope. Now they can anticipate a better day.*

*The Second Passenger has also restored communication. The signals are getting stronger every day. Help is on the way. Many of the remaining passengers hear the message loud and clear: "I will return. I will come again." Any day now those passengers who love Him expect to see that sudden burst of glory, that luminescent, iridescent cloud. They know what to look for. At first it is very small, and then it becomes a great celestial convoy. Redemption, salvation, rescue!*

Chapter 6

# "THEY SHALL SEE HIS FACE"

The Mediator accomplishes all that He sets out to do. The job description of Daniel 9:24 comes to mind: "To finish the transgression, and to make an end of sins, and to make reconciliation for iniquity, and to bring in everlasting righteousness." The gulf is bridged. The hostility is overcome. Peace and goodwill are established. Justice is done. The curse is entirely removed. Affliction shall not rise the second time. Once again the sons and daughters of God enjoy His presence unmediated. "They shall see his face" (Rev. 22:4).

Seventh-day Adventist theology is not patchwork. Our system of truth is integrative. The activity and ministry of the Mediator is its organizing principle. "In every school established the most simple theory of theology should be taught. In this theory, the atonement of Christ should be the great substance, the central truth. The wonderful theme of redemption should be presented to the students."—*Evangelism,* p. 223. "The student should learn to view the Word as a whole, and to see the relation of its parts. He should gain a knowledge of its grand, central theme, of God's original purpose for the world, of the rise of the great controversy, and of the work of redemption."—*Ibid.,* pp. 339, 340.

To understand the work of mediation and to follow the ministry of the Mediator means to enter into the plans and purposes of God—to attempt to think His thoughts after Him. Seventh-day Adventist theology, from this perspective, is seen to be supremely Christ-centered. He is mediator of creation, revelation, and redemption. He has everything to do with the affairs of Planet Earth. Without Him nothing exists. If He is not active, there is no communication with Heaven and no prospect of recovery from the fallout effects of Adam's defection. He is the axis on which the whole story turns. Jesus Christ as mediator is absolutely determinative. He becomes, as it were, the goal toward which all creation and redemption move. "Source, Guide, and Goal of all that is—to him be glory for ever! Amen" (Rom. 11:36, N.E.B.). We have just begun to grasp the deep significance of His words: "I am Alpha and Omega, the beginning and the end" (Rev. 22:13).

We now come to the ultimate state—complete restoration and reconciliation. Once again we can enjoy face-to-face communion with God. A communicating God created humanity for fellowship. He visited the first couple in Eden "in the cool of the day" (Gen. 3:8). Those times of fellowship were unmediated. They saw His face. His name was in their foreheads, that is, they reflected His character. So it must be again if mediation is to be complete.

That this fellowship should be broken for whatever reason pains our God. His great heart is restless until face-to-face communication is restored. The everlasting covenant was about peopling the earth with a holy, happy race. Not only would God be with each member of the human family, but He would be in them. "From eternal ages it was God's purpose that every created being, from the bright and holy seraph to man, should be a temple for the indwelling of the Creator."—*The Desire of Ages,* p. 161. Thwarted temporarily by the rebellion, this purpose is realized in the Incarnation. "And they shall call his name Emmanuel, which being interpreted is, God with us" (Matt. 1:23).

But even before the Incarnation—in fact, throughout Old Testament times—the Father intended to dwell among His people. For example, the sanctuary or tabernacle in the wilderness was constructed for this purpose. "And let them make me a sanctuary; that I may dwell among them" (Ex. 25:8). In another place the same idea is expressed as a promise to Israel: "Then there shall be a place which the Lord your God shall choose to cause his name to dwell there" (Deut. 12:11).

Other Scriptures in both the Old and New Testaments build on the concept. "For thus saith the high and lofty One that inhabiteth eternity, whose name is Holy; I dwell in the high and holy place, with him also that is of a contrite and humble spirit" (Isa. 57:15). Jesus and Paul took up the theme of a God who makes the human soul His dwelling place and the believing community His temple. "Even the Spirit of truth; . . . for he dwelleth with you, and shall be in you" (John 14:17). "For ye are the temple of the living God; as God hath said, I will dwell in them, and walk in them; and I will be their God, and they shall be my people" (2 Cor. 6:16).

The picture of a God who yearns for fellowship with His earthborn creatures comforts us and warms our hearts. The implications are far-reaching. Think what this does for the dignity of each human being! I am a person of such worth that the God of heaven wants to take up residence in me. Every person is a candidate for His occupancy. We are important to God and should therefore value ourselves as His blood-bought property. This idea places a high premium on humanity. It also places a real responsibility on every individual. "Know ye not that ye are the temple of God, and that the Spirit of God dwelleth in you? If any man defile the temple of God, him shall God destroy; for the temple of God is holy, which temple ye are" (1 Cor. 3:16, 17). But the indwelling referred to in these scriptures is not the ultimate. God envisions full restoration of face-to-face, unmediated association.

Some years ago evangelists frequently told the story of a New York newsboy. They called him an urchin. It was Christmas Eve. His mother was ill. He had no father. Having sold all his papers, he had just enough money to buy milk for his ailing mother. A bleak Christmas indeed. On the way home he looked wistfully into a beautifully decorated department store window. If only he could buy something for Mom. He pressed closer to the window—afraid to hope.

His eyes moistened.

The clerks were preparing the store for closing. People rushed by him, arms full of colorfully wrapped last-minute gifts. His nose was now almost on the glass. He was unaware that a tall, well-dressed man had been watching him. "How would you like to be able to give your mother that gift you are looking at, son?" The boy scarcely heard, so the man spoke a little louder, coming closer toward him.

"Sure would, mister, but there's no chance."

"Well, it's Christmas Eve, and I would like to do something for somebody. The spirit of the season, you know. Let me buy it before the store closes."

"Are you putting me on, mister?" the little fellow asked.

"No. Come, let's go in."

In less than ten minutes the gift was purchased, wrapped, and put in his hands. After thanking the kind man, the newsboy bounded down 34th Street holding his mother's gift tightly and saying over and over again, "I can't believe it. And there's no glass between!"

The Mediator must move the plan toward consummation. Access to the Father must become unrestricted, with "no glass between." All that He does in Creation, Incarnation, and every aspect of His atoning ministry is necessary. He could not miss one step in the process. Looking back over the total experience, we shall see that He is the way. "His right hand, and his holy arm, hath gotten him the victory" (Ps. 98:1). The way is now clear for the new creation. "And I saw a new heaven and a new earth: for the first heaven and the first earth were passed away; and there was no more sea" (Rev. 21:1).

The new creation begins with a new person created in Christ Jesus and constantly renewed by the Holy Spirit. It is consummated in a renovated planet with the Holy City, God's throne and dwelling place, as its capital. Heaven is a prepared place for prepared people (a phrase once used frequently in Adventism). Only those who choose to be there and who submit to the lordship of Christ can enter the city (chap. 22:14).

All those elements that would mar the new creation are excluded. In fact, they are annihilated. "But the fearful, and unbelieving, and the abominable, and murderers, and whoremongers, and sorcerers, and idolaters, and all liars, shall have their part in the lake which burneth with fire and brimstone: which is the second death" (chap. 21:8). Total extinction is the fate of the wicked.

Seventh-day Adventists stood almost alone in this belief for many years, but lately a number of respected Bible students have taken the same position. "The lake of fire is evidently a place of annihilation. . . . Not to be included in the book of life is the real end: these people disappear. With [Revelation] 20:11 one can say, 'And no place was found for them.' Revelation does not seem to know of any 'hell for sinners.' "—Edward Schillebeeckx, *Christ,* pp. 457, 458.

"John has allowed for the possibility that a man's name may be expunged from the book (Rev. 3:5), that human disobedience may in the end prove impregnable to the assaults of love. For such people the presence of God could be nothing but a horror from which they, like the earth they made their home, must flee, leaving not a trace behind. For them there remains only the annihilation of the second death."—G. B. Caird, *A Commentary on the Revelation of St. John the Divine,* p. 260.

The Mediator who was sent on a mission to seek and recover the lost planet returns the creation to its Father in all of its original beauty and splendor. There will be a definite act of rededication, of turning over the restored earth and its redeemed peoples to the commissioning God. "Then cometh the end, when he shall have delivered up the kingdom to God, even the Father; when he shall have put down all rule and all authority and power. For he must reign, till he hath put all enemies under his feet. The last enemy that shall be destroyed is death. For he hath put all things under his feet. But when he saith all things are put under him, it is manifest that he is excepted, which did put all things under him. And when all things shall be subdued unto him, then shall the Son also himself be subject unto him that put all things under him, that God may be all in all" (1 Cor. 15:24-28).

The Mediator identifies with those He came to seek and save. He is one of us. God did not lend Him, but He gave Him humanity. Jesus retains that humanness throughout eternity. He has permanently assumed what He came to redeem.

One striking fact about the new earth state is that it has no temple. The work of mediation has ended. Redeemed humanity will not need an intermediary. The saints "shall see his face" (Rev. 22:4). The impress of Deity is on them. (His name is in their foreheads.) "The man of the future" is a term coined by one writer to describe the people who will inherit the kingdom. It is so glorious that all the past fades into nothingness. God says, "I will create such a lovely earth that which was before will no longer be remembered or even come to mind."

The Mediator's work deals with real situations and with flesh-and-blood people. The results of Christ's mediatorial ministry are also real. We have spoken several times of the objective nature of salvation. The suffering creation itself is to be redeemed. Ellen White warns us of spiritualizing away the great realities of redemption. Real people, with real bodies, shall inhabit a new earth. The kingdom of glory is physical, tangible, literal, and glorious. At the Messianic banquet there is a real table with real fruit on it, and we shall be served by a real Person who can truly be called the Son of man because He is, in fact, one of us.

"The man of the future is like a child on Christmas Eve. He has asked for a model train and has pictured it to himself vividly with every detail and every possibility. But when he gets the long-awaited train on Christmas Eve, it is quite different. It is so beautiful that all earlier ideas about it are long since forgotten."—Schillebeeckx, *Christ,* p. 458.